HELP FROM ABOVE

BOOK ONE

"How I Went from Sweeping the
Floor to Painting the Sky"

DAVID ALAN ARNOLD

CONTENTS

INTRODUCTION

S OME DAYS YOU EAT THE bear…
Twelve thousand pounds of grizzly bears crowd the edge of an Alaskan salmon stream. Melted snow flows down the mountain into the bears' private sushi bar. The icy water shimmers with the vibration of our Bell 206 helicopter.

My pilot and I are the only humans for a hundred miles. But the bears don't look up at us. They stare at the stream, as if they'd just sat down after a long day and are reading a dinner menu.

"What kind of gun do you have?" I ask my pilot.

"Oh. I was just thinking about that…" he trails off. "I forgot to bring one."

Uh-oh. That's not good. The twelve killer beasts just woke up from hibernation and haven't eaten since last summer. Their massive stomachs are empty.

Every helicopter in Alaska is armed with heavy-caliber guns, because if you land, the bears will eat you alive. Many people have been mauled and eaten in the no-man's land beneath our skids. But *my* pilot forgot to bring a gun. So we have nothing to offer the bears, except tender human snacks.

I take a nervous breath. I've faced death before. But I've never seen so many claws and teeth ready to eat me if the engine quits. My throat tightens. Right now, I need every nut and bolt in this helicopter to keep me away from those hungry bears.

"You know what's weird? The salmon haven't started running yet…" my pilot observes matter-of-factly.

"What?" I gasp. There are no salmon in the salmon stream? If we have to land, we'll be surrounded by bears who haven't eaten since last year!

I nervously scan the engine gauges of our old 206 helicopter. The needles calmly point to little green arcs that assure me that all is well with our Allison C-20 Gas Turbine. And that's when I see it. The smallest needle on the panel fluctuates.

Did I really see that? Maybe I'm looking too hard at the gauge. Maybe I've mistaken normal helicopter vibration for a deadly drop in engine RPM.

There it is again! The tiny needle quivers. This small needle has a big job on our panel of gauges. Our engine is turning at fifty thousand RPM. But you can't make a gauge with fifty thousand numbers, so the little needle points to an exponential rate, while a big needle points to a healthy speed of fifty thousand.

The tiny needle is our canary in the coal mine. It warns us of danger we can't see or hear. Long before an engine failure shows on the big needle, the little needle indicates a loss of power. And now I'm staring at the little needle, just like the bears are staring at the empty salmon stream. To me and the bears, the needle and the stream are life.

Please little gauge…please stay where you are. But the gauge does not stay. It obeys Newton's Law. And to my horror, the tell-tale gauge begins to fall. My heart sinks as the little needle drops and makes a complete circle, all the way around to zero. Then it starts to spin backwards, circling down in a death-spiral. Our canary stops singing, and the Jet Ranger engine stalls. Suddenly, the big hand falls off the fifty thousand mark. I don't have time for words, just a single panic-stricken syllable. "Ooh!"

My pilot snaps his gaze to the engine gauges. Several of the needles slip out of the green and into bright red, warning us of death by gravity and bear claw.

There's no time to talk as we rise in our seatbelt straps. For a moment, we are weightless as the engine chokes and red warning lights flash. The noise of our gas turbine is replaced by the ear-splitting "Engine Out" horn. *BEEP! BEEP! BEEP!* the horn screams to warn us of what we already know — we're about to hit the ground at a hundred miles per hour.

Suddenly, the bears look up.

My pilot pulls his control levers, but the engine is dead. Instead of pulling us up into the sky, our helicopter falls toward the bears.

As we fall out of the sky and tumble to our doom, I'm struck by a solitary thought. *Nobody knows I'm here.* I've never told anyone what I do for work. My neighbors don't know that I'm flying in Alaska for NBC. No one knows that I'm clinging to life above a pack of hungry bears.

If I were smart, I would have written a book about my flying career. But I'm not smart. In fact, I've made a series of mistakes that ended up in this gravity-stricken helicopter. I stumbled into this situation without a plan to survive if something went wrong. My neighbors will have to read about my death in the newspaper, before they even know that I'm *in* Alaska.

I wish I could survive because someday, I want to have children. And those children will need someone to watch over them. I've always felt that I was cut out to be a father. But I guess it's not meant to be.

I tuck my head into the crash position as our helicopter falls out of the sky. I glance out my window and see a blurred picture of Earth, coming up to smash us. My stomach rises uncomfortably in my throat. My own choices brought me to this predicament. I've cheated death one too many times.

Welcome aboard my unusual journey. I can't promise you won't be crushed by gravity or eaten by bears. But I can promise you the adventure of a lifetime. Please fasten your seatbelt and brace for impact. My name is David Alan Arnold. And this is my story.

DOWN TO EARTH

"Any landing you walk away from is a good landing."

— *Unknown*

A S THE BELL HELICOPTER'S "ENGINE Out" alarm howls, I throw my Cineflex laptop control to the empty seat beside me. If we're crushed into a ball, I don't want the thing sitting on top of me.

It only takes a few seconds for us to fall out of the sky and hit the ground. Just before impact, my pilot pulls all the way up on his levers. I think he almost stops the blades with his Hail Mary pull. *WHAM!* as the heels of our skids smash into the rocks. This knocks us forward and blurs my vision as we somersault into the ground. *BANG!* as the toes of our skids hit. My pilot flails on his control levers in a Herculean effort to keep us from flipping upside-down on top of our main rotors. *WHOOSH-WHOOOSH-WHOOOOSH,* as he pulls every ounce of energy from the 206's main rotors.

As we cartwheel across the tundra, I brace for what I know is next, the main rotors tearing themselves apart against the unforgiving Alaska ground. But, miraculously, my pilot wrestles the aircraft upright, and we bounce through bear country on our skids. I know I have guardian angels, because the helicopter stays in one piece.

We *should* be dead, but we're not. Our helicopter should be smashed, but it comes to a sliding stop on its skids, with the "Engine Out" alarm screaming as loud as a New York taxi's horn. But I don't care. I'm so glad to be alive, I could kiss my pilot, even though he's a burly Alaskan bush pilot. He climbs out of his seat and works quickly to repair the failed engine before the bears realize that a can of human sardines has landed next to their unpopulated salmon stream.

I don't see any bears yet, but I *know* they saw us crash next to their empty fishing spot.

Lucky for us, the problem with our flying machine is a simple one, and it takes my pilot less than ten minutes to repair it. Confident we're not dead yet, he presses the starter button on the Jet Ranger. *Tick-Tick-Tick-BOOM!* The starter/generator sends sparks into a fuel-air mixture inside the Allison C-20's 'hot' section. There's an explosion, and the powerful turbine spins back to a deafening roar of fifty thousand RPM. He pulls up on his collective lever, and we surge into the sky.

Once again, we're looking down at the starving bears. But as we climb to a thousand feet, the engine out alarm screams again. Our eyes snap to the instrument cluster, where gauges wobble red and then surge back into the green. I share a grateful glance with my pilot. We're never out of harm's way in our office. I'm grateful for every day I'm still alive. Everyone has problems at work, but some days I'm just glad if I don't get eaten by bears.

OUT OF THE CRIB, INTO THE SKY

I wasn't always a Hollywood helicopter cameraman. I started out as a scared little boy.

One of my earliest memories is of my mom. "What's wrong sweet heart?" she asks, knowing full-well.

"I heard you and dad fighting and slamming things," I whimper through my toddler tears.

Mom takes a tense breath. "I know sweetheart. Sometimes daddy and I argue, but we always love you."

Mom is a busy grownup, but she doesn't just dry my tears and shoo me along. She sits right by my side and combs my hair neatly to the side with her fingers.

Mom says I'm "sensitive." Even at age five, I have difficulty accepting things that don't bother anyone else. But mom always seeks me out and takes the time to sit with me and talk about it. She dries my tears and asks why I'm upset, even when she knows the answer. Mom drops everything and comforts me, doesn't judge me, doesn't tell me to get over it...she just loves me.

Years earlier, at the tender age of three years old, I stand in my crib, gripping the bars like a prison inmate, and stare out the window, waiting for mom to enter the driveway and come home from work.

While waiting for her, I have a very strange sensation, and I float up out of my crib. Even at three, I know this isn't right. I squeeze the bars of my crib and try to force my feet back onto the mattress, but I can't hold on. I float up over the bars of my crib and, to my horror, I fly through the window, out of the house, into the front yard.

7

Being lifted into the air is terrifying to a three-year-old. I scream, but nothing comes out. Now I'm turning above the driveway. The roof passes under my feet, and I'm pulled over the top of the house. Although my recollection is crystal clear, it ends abruptly, as I float over the roof and leave our family home. I have no memory of what comes next. If it was a dream, I must have awakened. If it wasn't a dream, I don't know...

I have a strange relationship with the laws of nature.

Flying comes back into my life at age 22. I'm a grownup now, and I want to fly—but not like a normal person in an airplane. I just want to fly. With every fiber of my being, I want to rise above the trees and see what's up there. Maybe I want to finish my toddler experience and see above the roof this time. It's a ridiculous wish, but I can't let it go. I don't know how to describe this weird fixation, except that I wish for it with all my might.

I found George Lucas's biography, *Skywalking*. There's a copy of the book in the library of my little hometown of Brooksville, Florida. Lucas' story of growing up in his little town and making his way in the movie business shows me a path I can follow.

I love *Skywalking*. It's the story of a man who found a way to make his mark on the world. George Lucas' *Star Wars* movies revolutionized the world of film. Small-town life in Brooksville, FL has no connection to Hollywood, but I know if George Lucas can do it, then so can I.

But there's one thing I can't figure out in *Star Wars*. In the climax of Episode IV, Luke Skywalker has to hit a tiny target with a torpedo to save the world, but before he shoots, a voice tells him to turn off his targeting computer. That makes no sense. How can you hit the target without seeing it? Somehow, George Lucas made it work. Luke hits his target and blows up the Death Star. Everyone lives happily ever after. That's good enough for me. And it's a good metaphor for a kid in Florida who wants to work in Hollywood but can't see what he's aiming at.

I don't have good grades or enough money to go to USC film school like George Lucas. So I move to Melbourne, FL to take film classes at a junior college. I take on the challenge of learning my new career with the force of a hurricane, working on every school film project I can find.

After a year, I drop out of school to begin work in the movie business. I remember a school official mocking me in front of other students. "How far do you think you're going to get without a college degree?" That's a fair question. I don't really have a plan.

But I work hard and manage to make enough money to scrape by in a town that has very little film and TV work. There is so little work in Melbourne, FL, that I'm often asked how I can earn a living. One of my tricks is to visit every company in the phone book that advertises Film and Television. There's almost no work, but I just keep hustling.

I suppose it can be annoying to get regular visits from a guy looking for work. The guy at the front counter is polite, but blunt. "Quit coming around here; we have no use for you." So I respectfully scratch his company off my list.

But the same company calls me three weeks later. I haven't visited since they told me to quit coming around, but now they're calling me? I suppose there's a lesson here. Because I'd been coming around and keeping in touch, they thought of me when they suddenly needed someone. That's how I was called to interview with Ed Silva, Vice President of Wescam, USA.

Ed's building doesn't say "Wescam" on the sign out front. It says CRM Group, a company known for film and video production. I've never heard of Wescam. I have no idea what a Wescam is, or what Ed and his people do.

Ed says, "Why don't you come out and see one of our crews in action?" So I drive to the Melbourne Airport and meet Wescam guys David Norris and Dan Kelley. They're attaching a camera onto a helicopter for a Hollywood movie.

Amazing! Here I am in Melbourne, FL, which is as far away from Hollywood as you can get, and I'm watching David and Dan work on a big Hollywood movie. Silva says he can hire an experienced film cameraman from the Hollywood or New York movie business to work alongside David and Dan, but he's considering me because he likes using local people.

He looks at me thoughtfully and says, "You look hungry...are you hungry?" And with that, he closes the interview. "I'll make my decision of who I'll hire in the next day or two..." he says while showing me the door.

Ed's right. I am hungry. But I'm not just hungry. I'm starving! In my humble Melbourne apartment, I stare at the cardboard box that holds my tiny TV off the floor. My TV is the size of a dinner plate. Most of my furniture came from dumpster-diving. But I'm thinking about the amazing job at Wescam. How can I convince Ed to hire *me* instead of one of the big shots from Hollywood or New York? I'm a nobody, and I don't know anything about the crazy machines they use at Wescam. I don't know anything about helicopters, but I know I want that job.

Dumping the trash at my apartment, I see an old work boot in the dumpster. That gives me an idea. That filthy stinking boot is perfect!

I dive into the dumpster with the enthusiasm of a gold-miner digging up the mother-lode and grab the old dirty boot. I put the slimy oil-soaked work boot on a dinner plate and snap a picture of myself carving into it like a sirloin steak. I smile as if I'm about to eat the best meal ever.

I carefully roll a sheet of paper into my typewriter, pound out an enthusiastic letter to Ed, paste the picture of me eating my boot to it, and deliver it to Ed's office.

Ed hires me on the spot. "Hungry" indeed.

Ed Silva gives me my first big break. And what he offers me is the thing I've always wanted — to fly.

It's an amazing job, flying for television and movies, with a technology Wescam developed to smooth out helicopter vibration. Their cameras don't shake and vibrate like other helicopter cameras; the Wescam lens floats smoothly through the air.

Wescam gimbals are complicated machines with gyroscopes, onboard computers, and delicate electrical connections that require expert repairs. But I know nothing of aircraft, gyros, or repairs. I can't fix anything, especially if Steven Spielberg is screaming at me to get the thing working. So I decide to stay up until 2:00 am each night, teaching myself about electronics and movie cameras.

I read Wescam tech manuals into a tape recorder and listen to the books over and over until I fall asleep. Soon, I can quote the technical books like Bible chapters.

At first, my coworkers are annoyed with my lack of knowledge. But I'm studying the books so hard they start bringing me parts from the Wescam System, so I can help them figure out what the parts are called. The guys have a common name for each part of the machine, but you can't call a military factory and order a "doo-hickey" to fix the "springy part." You have to know the military part name.

I've read the book so many times that they can show me a doo-hickey and I can tell them whether it's a "Dome-Vehicle Interface" or "Lateral Isolator," even if I've never seen one before. I'm still a new guy, but I'm hungry.

Ed Silva opened the door to movies and TV shows. Wherever I go in my career, it's because Ed Silva gave me a big break when I was a hungry kid from the streets.

Fox Sports
Super Bowl 51

SWEEPING THE FLOOR

SOMETIMES PEOPLE ASK HOW I ended up with a high-tech career. "Did you go to school for this?"

No. I didn't go to school for this. I don't have a college degree. All I have is hard work, without complaint.

So I started sweeping the floor at Wescam. No one told me to sweep the floor, but with everyone out working on movies and TV shows, the shop is a little dirty. Actually, the shop is a mess. The guys spend most of their time on location with the half-million-dollar Wescam gyro-stabilized cameras, so they don't have time to clean the shop. Piles of dirt, debris, and strange-looking parts are everywhere.

So, I start sweeping. I sweep until the entire floor of the massive shop is clean. That takes until about 2:00 am. Then, I start straightening and organizing the piles of parts. It's an endless task. I don't know what the aerospace gadgets are, so I just organize them as best I can. Instead of heaping piles of junk on every workbench, I leave a clean workbench where someone can work on a Wescam system.

When the sun rises on the office, I'm still here, wearing the same clothes I had on yesterday, sweeping and straightening. I suppose the place is barely recognizable. My boss David Norris walks in, takes one look at the neat, organized shop and points at me victoriously. "You're going with me on my next shoot." I didn't ask him to take me on his next shoot, but he knows I'm hungry and willing to work. So he rewards my overnight sweep-a-thon with an on-the-spot promotion.

I'll never forget the feeling of being lifted off the ground in the helicopter with David Norris and his Model 36 Wescam. It's not violent or overwhelming, like I thought it would be. When our pilot, Al Guthrie, pulls on the collective of his Aerospatiale TwinStar, the twin Allison engines smoothly apply power to the blades, and we float off the ground, into the sky.

In that moment, my crazy dream of flying comes true as we float up over the tree tops.

They say you shouldn't look down from great heights, but I'm looking down. The people and cars and houses are getting smaller as Al and the TwinStar lift us a thousand feet above Earth. I can see the entire city below, every building, every rooftop, every person, as the population of an entire human city swarms below our skids.

DEAD MAN'S CURVE

O NE DAY, I WALK INTO the Wescam office and find my coworkers in a somber mood. The normally upbeat guys look shaken, as if someone has died. David Norris pulls me aside and says that a helicopter crashed, and one of our colleagues has been killed.

I notice that the expert technicians at Wescam share a reverence for the unforgiving laws of physics that have taken the life of one of our peers. It could've been any of us.

The Wescam guys are experts in helicopter vortex ring state and height-velocity diagrams. But I'm new, and I don't really understand the science of flight. I don't know the merciless killers that stalk us during every camera flight.

Apparently, when you're soaring just above the tree-tops, death can come swiftly. I listen closely when the Wescam guys speak of a close call with death or an accident that took the life of a colleague.

"What's the 'Dead Man's Curve?'" I ask Norris. He eyes me thoughtfully and takes a deep breath. Norris explains that helicopters normally fly high enough to safely land if the engine quits. But with our cameras, flying at tree-top level for movies and television, we're too low to get away safely. We're going to crash in a twisted shitpile if anything goes wrong.

A height-velocity diagram shows when a helicopter can safely land, and when it will crash and burn. That thin line shows the safe and the deadly side of the curve. Our side of the line is known as "The Dead Man's Curve."

Have you ever heard that "numbers don't lie"? These numbers

will kill you. It's simple math and only a matter of time before your number is up.

Norris is a very smart man. He looks at me thoughtfully and pushes his eyeglasses firmly against his forehead. "You know Dave, not many men make a long career out of this..."

I KNOW SHE CAN HEAR YOU

L IFE IS GOOD. WORK IS amazing.

I'm so obsessed with my career at Wescam that I routinely work 90 hours a week and rarely take time to visit friends or family. If I make plans to see them, I often cancel or don't show up.

I'm not a good son, and I miss several planned visits to my mom in Brooksville. Although my mom always spent time with me when I was little, I'm too busy to visit her now. That's not OK. And one day my mom's boyfriend, Klaus, calls because I'm cancelling again. Something's wrong. He sounds serious and says, "You need to come."

I don't know it yet, but my mom is in the hospital. When I arrive, Klaus says she's very sick with cancer and is not going to make it. A few days ago, she went to the hospital because her back was hurting. When they ran tests, they discovered the cancer had grown throughout her body. It's in her organs and her bones. There is nothing they can do. She *will* die, and soon.

The doctor explains I'm about to lose my mom. I can see her through the glass, lying peacefully in her hospital bed as we talk about her. They say the death will be swift and it's certain; it can't be stopped.

I'm devastated. My mom is the one who comforts me. She always takes time to hear about my feelings and make me feel loved. At age 25, I'd never considered my mom's mortality. I don't know what to do.

I open the door to her room. I'm trying to be strong, but I can't hide my fear. My mom is sick and tired but, as usual, she comforts me.

Tears are pouring down my face as we hug. She pats me on the back and says, "We'll get through this." How can she say that? She's talking about her own death.

I'm afraid to lose my mom, but I'm floored by her strength. My mom is a strong, classy lady. I say, "I love you," through my tears. "Every good part of me comes from you…" My mom cries too as we hug. Those are the last words we ever share.

The hospital is a nice place, but cold and antiseptic. I want my mom to feel comfort and love, so I buy a stereo for her room and play music from a composer she likes.

The nurses smile as the monochrome drone of the hospital is replaced with the sound of music. I don't think this is allowed. Maybe they're allowing me to break the rules because mom's dying and could use a little comfort.

When I talk to my boss at Wescam, I can't keep it together to explain what's happening. I think, through the sobs, he can understand that my mom is dying. David Norris is a caring man and asks, "Is your family there?"

I lie and say, "Yeah. I have people here."

My mom is *so* sick with cancer the doctors give her massive amounts of pain medications. The drugs put her into a coma. She can't be awakened. This begins the most painful chapter of my life. Mom doesn't awaken from her drug-induced coma, and I haven't been able to talk to her since I first saw her in the hospital.

Her illness is so sudden that most of my family doesn't have time to visit and say goodbye before she passes. I'm one of the lucky ones. People have unfinished business with my mom. But at least I got to talk to her one last time before her death.

A voice in my head tells me to call grandma and put her on the phone with mom. That makes no sense, because mom's in a coma. She can't talk. But this voice won't quit.

I'm a sane person, but the voice is telling me to do something crazy. I once saw a wild-eyed homeless man waving his arms and talking to the voice in his head as he stumbled down the street. I felt sorry for him. But if I'm honest, I have to admit there's only a thin line between us. I hear voices, too.

Grandma can't come to visit, and I know mom will die any day now. The little voice says I need to put her on the phone with mom *right now*. So I call grandma and talk about the strange idea. "Grandma, I'm going to put the phone next to mom and, if you want, you can talk to her. Mom can't talk to you, but I know she can hear you."

I don't know if mom can hear anything. But the voice says to put mom and grandma on the phone. I place the phone next to my mom's ear and sit there with no idea of how to conduct this strange meeting. The room is still. The only sound is mom's cancer-stricken breath. But the silence is broken by a soft sound from the phone receiver. Grandma starts talking. A long time passes in this one-way conversation. My mom doesn't move a muscle, just lays there, silent, eyes shut. But grandma goes on and on, talking to her. I don't know what this is, but it feels important.

Grandma talks for quite a while. I guess she had a lot to say to her daughter. When she finally goes quiet I pick up the phone. "Hi, Grandma."

"Hi sweetie." Grandma sounds relieved, as if a burden has been lifted.

This unthinkable phone call causes a stir in our family. Some of the women say they're amazed I thought to do this for grandma. But I didn't think of it. I'm a young, self-absorbed fool. I don't know where the voice came from, but I'm glad my grandma got to connect with her daughter before her death. Thank God I listened to the voice.

Cancer is cruel and merciless. I watch as it steals the life from my beautiful mom. I hold her hand as she takes her last, painful breaths…and is gone.

People who know me say I'm a ridiculously happy person. But after mom dies, I'm terribly depressed for the first time in my life. I can't shake the blanket of sorrow that consumes me day and night. One night I cry so hard, I can't breathe. I'm being crushed by sadness and a longing to see my mom again.

It doesn't help that night after night, I dream that mom is alive.

I'm so happy in my dream. Her sickness and death are no more. She's back.

"Hello sweetie," she says. Her smile lights up the room. "Go get Peaches (our little lapdog). We're going to give her a haircut."

Seeing mom alive and healthy is like seeing the sunrise at the end of a terrible night. We talk and laugh as we corral our little dog, who DOES NOT want a haircut. I'm so happy to have mom back and to spend time with her.

But there's a noise somewhere in the house. Instantly, I know we're in danger, and we have to get out of here.

"Mom! We gotta go."

But mom can't hear me. Maybe it's the sound of the hair clippers she's running through Peaches' fur. She's intently focused on our cute little dog. The hallway to my childhood room is darkened by a shadow. Something monstrous is coming.

"Mom! We have to get out of here!"

Mom pauses from haircutting. She looks up, but can't understand what I'm saying. I glance at the hallway. It's completely darkened by the shadow of a huge monster. There can be no escape.

I awaken. The room of my apartment is empty. There's no one here. It's just me. Mom died a month ago. It was just a dream that she's alive. And now, I'm awake.

Another night when I go to sleep, the light is back. Mom is alive again, and it's like awakening from a nightmare. I'm relieved and overjoyed. We're back in my childhood home.

"What kind of sandwich do you want, sweetie?" my mom asks as she puts peanut butter and jelly on a slice of whole wheat bread.

"Why did you ask that?" I say, pointing to the open jar of peanut butter. But mom says nothing. She knows what kind of sandwich I like, and she's already making it.

I look through the kitchen of my childhood home. It feels so good to be back here with my mom. But there's something on the floor that doesn't belong here. Is that a coil of rope? The pattern of colors are hypnotic. What is it?

I suddenly realize that there's an eastern diamondback

rattlesnake on the floor of our kitchen. The snake isn't moving, just staring intently at mom's ankle.

"Mom! Look out! There's a snake!"

"What?" Mom can't understand me, even though I'm right beside her, screaming.

The snake pulls its head back like an archer. Its tail twitches violently with the murderous sound of the rattle.

"Mom! Get out of here! There's a snake!"

Now mom looks up from the sandwich. "What?" She still doesn't understand what I'm saying.

"Mom! Look out!"

But mom's not looking at the snake; she's looking at me, and she steps back away from me, closer to the spring-loaded viper on the floor. But mom doesn't see the snake.

Suddenly, I'm not in my child-hood home. I'm in my apartment. There's no one here, just me. I was so upset about the snake biting mom I woke myself up.

But mom died two months ago. It was just a dream that she's alive again. I look around my empty apartment. It's never felt so cold. Mom is gone. I'm sitting upright in bed, covered in sweat and hyperventilating. My dream is over and for the sixtieth time, I've awakened to a world without mom. A suffocating blanket of sadness comes over me with a soul-sucking darkness. It's a darkness I can *feel*. Each night when I go to sleep I get my mom back, only to lose her again when I awaken.

Out of my darkness comes a ridiculous wish. It's sort of like my wish of flying. It makes no sense, but I want something impossible. I want to talk to mom again. It's madness, but I can't let go. I want it, the way a man dying of thirst wants a glass of water.

YOUR MOM IS HERE

DONNA MCMAHON IS THE MOTHER of one of my childhood friends. Her son Jason and I attended Cub Scouts together. After my mom's death, Donna became like a second mom to me. We talk all the time, and we talk about everything. Donna is salty and outspoken, and she will tell me exactly what she thinks with no filter.

But Donna's on the phone and seems out of sorts. She usually talks without sugar-coating. But she's struggling to find words. "I don't know how to tell you this, but your mom is here."

"Ummm. What?"

"Your mom has been hanging around. She's with me all the time. She's here now."

Mom died months ago. This is the strangest thing I have ever heard. And it's coming from the most no-nonsense person I know. Neither of us know what to do. My mom can't be here. She's dead. But Donna is sure that my mom is with her.

"Hmmm." I say. "Really?"

"Yeah. I know it sounds weird, honey. I don't understand this. But I think I'm supposed to tell you about it."

"What should we do?"

Donna takes a deep breath. "I don't know honey. But I think I'm supposed to tell you that she's here."

I'm stunned. Is it really happening? How is this possible? What should we do? And then a thought becomes clear.

"OK. I am going to ask you a question that my mom would know, and you wouldn't."

This will be easy. Donna didn't know my mom.

I say, "Myrna?"

Donna says, "Sister!"

My Aunt Myrna has never visited here. Donna doesn't know that mom had a sister named Myrna.

Wow! This *is* really happening. My mom *is* here.

I let out a huge breath. A lifetime of tension leaves my body. I slump into the couch in my apartment. My mom didn't cease to exist when the cancer took her. She's still here. And, as usual, she's taking time to comfort me. Death is final, but my mom loves me enough to bend the rules to spend time with me, like she always has.

I ask the obvious questions. "Is mom OK?" "Is she in pain?" "What is she saying?"

"She's fine sweetie. She's not in any pain. But she's worried about you."

Wow. I'm amazed as a wave of comfort washes over me, although I'm confused by what she says next. "Honey, she wants to warn you of trouble ahead—something to do with a book." Shortly after that, she hangs up. Although the warning is puzzling, the call leaves me feeling better.

Have you ever lost someone you couldn't let go of? If you're like me and you've felt someone watching over you and helping, it might be them.

I've spent my career careening through the sky, sometimes miles above the clouds, sometimes inches above the ocean, rocketing at a hundred miles an hour. Since mom died, I've done a lot of dangerous things, but I felt guided and protected at every turn. My pilots and I have gotten lost in blizzards, tumbled to the ocean, veered into deadly power lines. Yet each time I've been helped and protected from Mother Nature and the unforgiving laws of physics that have often killed my colleagues.

NAZCA

THIS MORNING, THE NATIONAL NEWSPAPER in Peru ran a headline that included me and the national heritage of Peru. The headline says, "Nazca Lines Destroyed by Helicopter." That's bad news. Even worse, I was in the helicopter.

I'm in Peru to film a commercial with a helicopter that's owned by an Air Force general.

But we are not filming. At this moment my colleagues, the director and producer of the cell phone commercial, are locked in a Peruvian Prison, along with our helicopter pilot.

The Nazca Lines are fantastic ancient ruins that rival the Egyptian Pyramids in wonder and mystery. They're miles long, perfectly shaped, and can only be seen from high above the Earth, but they were built *thousands* of years before the Wright brothers lifted the first humans high enough to see them.

We know what crop circles look like because we can fly high enough above them to see that the trampled corn makes a shape. But the Nazca Lines are even bigger. You have to fly a mile high to see the shapes sprawling to the horizon.

Here's the kicker. These magic drawings in the sand have survived thousands of years, because there's no wind in the ancient Peruvian desert.

Thousands of years ago a lost civilization drew lines in the sand that stretch for miles across the desert. The artists must have had advanced math and engineering to create the massive shapes, and they did so before Jesus was born. But the ancient wizards vanished from the face of the Earth; no one knows who they were or where they went.

The ancient drawings make modern crop circles look like child's play. We don't even know how they made them at a time when the people of Earth did not have technology to fly high enough to see them.

I first saw the lines through the flickering mechanical shutter of our Wescam gyro-stabilized movie camera, from five thousand feet above the Earth. That's how high we had to climb in our helicopter to see the lines.

Unfortunately, our helicopter makes wind to rise above the ancient sand drawings. And wind blows away sand.

One of the fragile drawings is actually the national symbol of Peru. Being dusted-off and erased by a foreign helicopter is akin to terrorists destroying the Statue of Liberty.

I have a giant problem. And, as usual, I have no plan to get out of this mess.

I've blundered my way into doomsday, and I can't think of a way to escape. Right now, I'm in a restaurant, with two big, scary-looking men sitting across from me, not eating, just staring at me with murder in their eyes.

Because of the newspaper headlines, everyone in Peru thinks I've destroyed their national heritage. I'm pretty sure I don't have long to live.

The newspapers are wrong. Our helicopter didn't harm the Nazca Lines. But corrupt officials and journalists said we destroyed the Nazca Lines and blew away the national symbol of Peru with our helicopter. I don't know why they printed it, but I know that in a crime-ridden ghetto, it doesn't matter what really happened, just what corrupt officials and murderous thugs can get away with.

If the entire country believes I've destroyed their national heritage, the bad guys can do anything they want to me. Even though I've done nothing wrong, my imprisonment and death will be applauded by Peruvians everywhere.

My life is worth less here than the Wescam gyro-stabilized camera, which will probably be stolen by the people at the next table in the restaurant. They just keep staring at me, not talking, not eating. I'd expect people to stare at me that way if I'd killed their children.

I called the U.S. Embassy last night and told an official that I'm the one in the newspaper. The official took a breath and asked, "Do you know how much trouble you're in?" Her tone suddenly sounded like she's talking to a condemned man on death row.

"Yes," I say nervously.

I figure, since we all agree that I'm in trouble, they can escalate the US Government response and save me from this corrupt, third-world mess. After all, I didn't destroy anything. The Nazca Lines weren't harmed.

But the Embassy Official says something that takes my breath away. "We can't rescue you. All we can do is document whatever they do to you."

"Whatever they do?" That sounds like they can do "whatever they want" and my government won't lift a finger to protect me.

My heart sinks. Nothing can save me. I'm doomed—I'm public enemy number one in a third-world country where I don't speak the language enough to order a cup of coffee. I'm certainly not going to talk my way out of criminal charges before a corrupt Spanish-speaking firing squad.

I can't think of a way to save my skin, and this time, I've out-done myself. I thought it was a good idea to stay behind to look after the camera equipment when the rest of the film crew fled the country. And I thought it was wise to travel with no money or ID, since they can be stolen on the nearly-lawless streets of Peru. So I have no way to even pay for a bus ticket out of the desert, where bad guys are likely plotting my death and dividing up my camera equipment.

People like me usually just disappear after a thing like this. You might see a flash on the news like, "Cameraman Kidnapped, Feared Dead in Peru."

I have to escape, but to physically run across the Peruvian desert with no money, food or water, is certain death. But I'd actually prefer it to death in a Peruvian prison.

Right now, my life looks like the season finale of *Locked Up Abroad*.

Trying to appear casual, I rise from my seat and slip away from the scary-looking thugs. I'm pretending not to panic as I move toward the hotel exit. If I can slip out of town, I can begin my walk across the desert. Hopefully, by some miracle I can avoid prison or murder and walk out of Peru.

"Excuse me señor!" There's nothing worse than polite words spoken in furious anger.

The man at the front desk is blocking my exit, as the scary-looking guys move in behind me. I am surrounded by angry men.

"How are you going to pay?!" asks the clerk, who is staring at me like a piece of meat.

I'm speechless. I didn't expect the hotel to demand money before I can leave. I don't have any money.

But that's OK. I have an easy answer. The film company always pays the hotel bill for the crew. Swallowing the lump in my throat, I speak as if nothing is wrong. "The company will pay."

The look on this guy's face says I might be murdered in the lobby. "No señor. They did not pay. You're the last one here. You will have to pay for all the rooms before you can leave."

Shit! The producer skipped town without paying the hotel bill for any of the crew. Did I mention I'm an idiot? I don't have two nickels, or pesos, or whatever they pay with here. I can't escape Peru. I can't even escape the hotel. The hotel guy shoots a glance to the scary-looking thugs, and they move closer with clenched fists.

I've blundered before, but this time I've out-done myself, and I can see the walls closing in. I'm surrounded by thugs with murder in their eyes. They swarm between me and the door, blocking my escape. Compared to the thugs, a thousand miles of barren desert on the other side of the door looks inviting. But I can't get to the hot desert sands that might allow me to live one more day. The men in this room won't let me leave.

As the thugs move closer, a voice comes from nowhere, "Hello. I'm Maria Reich." I turn to find a graceful lady extending her hand. "Tell me what happened to the Nazca Lines." The thugs take a step back. Maria seems to have some influence here.

"Tell me what happened," she repeats, the way a mother would comfort a small child.

"We flew over the Nazca Lines, but never got near them. We didn't disturb anything. We never got close enough to the lines to hit them with wind from our helicopter," I say.

She listens thoughtfully and says, "OK. Don't worry. There is old damage to the lines from a terrorist attack years ago. I'm going to inspect the lines. We'll straighten this out." She turns and walks out to a waiting Peruvian Air Force helicopter.

The murderous thugs vanish into the woodwork of the old hotel. Apparently, Maria is a powerful figure here, and I have come under her protection.

Maria takes to the sky in the military helicopter and flies over the lines to inspect the damage. She must have said good things, because immediately my pilot is released from prison, and I'm released from the hotel. Maria, it turns out, is a very influential Peruvian dignitary. Her mother discovered the Nazca Lines.

Our commercial producer didn't get permission from authorities to film the National Heritage of Peru and threw Maria's name around, saying that Maria approved our flight over the Nazca Lines. Maria said she did no such thing, and our little production got her into hot water with authorities. We caused a huge problem for Maria when our producer fouled her reputation.

Maria had every reason to let me rot in Peruvian jail after our stupid stunt made her look bad, and we got ourselves onto the front page of the National Newspaper of Peru as terrorists who destroyed the Nazca Lines. But today, she's going out of her way to get me off the hook and save me from a nationwide lynch-mob.

Everything opens up as I come under Maria's protection. Even the unpaid hotel bill is no longer a problem, so I can leave and fly in the helicopter back to the Capital City of Lima and on to freedom and safety in the United States.

God bless Maria Reiche. I did nothing to deserve rescue. But she went out of her way to save me. If you think that sounds crazy, get used to it. This is the story of my life — blundering into trouble and being rescued by friends or a complete stranger who has every reason to let me die in prison.

I'll never forget how great it felt to be on that plane ride back to the United States of America, where people aren't killed or imprisoned without due process. When people kiss the ground on arrival, I know why. When you've been to countries where your life is worth less than a hundred dollars, the United States is Heaven on Earth.

THE WRONG STUFF

I'M LIVING MY DREAM OF floating above the trees. I'm flying for some of the biggest TV shows and movies. But it's not a complete triumph on my part. Sometimes I screw up.

There's a scene in the movie *Armageddon* where a NASA pilot looks at the motley crew of oil workers chosen to fly into space to save the world. It's a funny scene, where the blue-collar oil workers stumble clumsily in their space suits. A highly-trained NASA pilot complains bitterly about "The Wrong Stuff..."

I was on the movie crew at NASA when that scene was filmed, and I'm staring at a thousand feet of exposed film hanging from our helicopter camera.

I'm not supposed to be able to see the film. In fact, the priceless movie film has to be carefully handled to prevent accidental exposure to light. But here I am, looking at a neatly wound roll of film, in broad daylight, because I forgot which magazine has the exposed film and, stupidly, I opened the wrong one.

Movie pilot Alan Purwin and Cinematographer Kurt Soderling have been flying that camera around a NASA Space Shuttle for the movie. And I just ruined the entire roll of film, like an idiot. I want to die.

But I'm not done screwing up. As we're trying to figure out what to do about the ruined film and lost scenes, we suddenly realize I also locked the keys inside our van, which is now blocking the Space Shuttle.

NASA wants us to move the van, but we're stuck because while ruining the footage, I locked the keys inside, so we have no way to move it.

Kurt looks at me in stunned disbelief. How could anyone be

so stupid? How is it possible to mess up everything all at once? I acknowledge my only reasonable option by preparing to slash my wrists with the scissors I keep in my fanny-pack. I really want to die.

But Kurt doesn't fault me or fire me. Instead, he swings into action and takes responsibility for every mistake I made. He meets with the movie director and head cameraman and tells them that we ruined the film together.

Kurt had nothing to do with my unforgivable error, but he took the blame for it. Next, he hunts around and finds a member of the crew who knows how to break into cars. I watch in amazement as the man disables the driver's door lock with disturbing ease. He pops open the door so we can get the keys and move the van before it becomes a National Security incident next to the Space Shuttle.

Kurt doesn't say a word about my idiot disaster, just tells me to reload the camera and get back to work. Kurt stood up for me, even though I was horribly in the wrong, and he taught me important lessons. He showed me how to be a responsible leader and how to handle your crew's mistakes. He also taught me that when you mess up, you still deserve a helping hand. Wherever I go in life, I'll be a better person because of the way Kurt Soderling treated me on the worst day of my working life.

History Channel
Ice Road Truckers

History Channel
Axe Men

CBS
The Amazing Race

MAY GOD BLESS FOOLS

FLYING ABOVE THE TREETOPS IS surreal. I feel like a god, floating over the city, looking down on the people of Earth, living their lives. They only see what's right in front of them as they toil at their jobs and drive in their cars. But up here I can see what they cannot. They are part of a giant hive of humanity.

I'm eye-level with their hundred-floor offices. I see them, sitting at desks, working in cubicles. I'm just like them, but up here I can look down on millions of people all at once, walking, working, and driving in a spectacular symphony of human life. My camera takes in a godlike view as we paint every living spirit in the city.

But I'm not a god. I'm a human, sitting in an imperfect machine, built by flawed people and flown by human pilots. I worry about what may come when human error takes us down a notch.

Some of my colleagues have died in my seat. We live like Sky Kings, above the people of Earth, but death is a split-second away. Sometimes, when I take my eye off the perfect Wescam gyro-stabilized image, I look outside the aircraft and see death staring back at me.

"Cable!" I yell in Spanish at my South American pilot. The pilot snaps his gaze to the end of my pointing finger to find the power lines as they go into our main rotor blades. The laws of physics are a brutal bitch in moments like this. Our pilot was so distracted by the car we're filming he forgot to look where he was going. He avoids hitting the wires, but his emergency pull causes us to tumble out of control. Our guardian angels keep us in one piece. I know I have help from above as the aircraft rumbles to a stop in a cloud of South American dust. My pilot looks at me sheepishly. *"Tu eres un buen copiloto."* He shakes my hand, grateful to be alive. And he's right. If I hadn't yelled at him and called his attention to the wires as he flew into them, the wires would have stopped our blades and balled us to a fiery death. I'm lucky to be alive.

Back in Los Angeles, I explain the pilot error to a movie pilot named Rick Shuster. Rick is an awesome camera pilot. I'm sure he'll have some clever insight into the mishap, but he offers not a word of comfort. Instead, he stares at me like a piece of meat. His brow furrows and he says something that takes my breath away, "What were you doing in that helicopter?"

"Well, I was operating the camera."

"No. That's not what I'm asking. If the pilot is messing up, why didn't you tell him to land and let you out?"

Shit. That's not what I want to hear. It hurts my feelings because Rick is right. I'd seen enough signs of trouble I should have quit flying with the inexperienced pilot before he made his near-deadly mistake. I'm partly to blame for the problem, because I should have known better than to sit quietly while our pilot made one mistake after another, until we finally hit the ground in a cloud of dust. That flight should have killed me.

Ugh. Rick's right. I thought I could point the righteous finger of blame to my hapless pilot, but if I'm honest, I must admit that I helped put myself into harm's way. Typical.

Why do my stories begin and end with me doing something stupid? Thank God for my guardian angels. If I didn't have help from above, I'd be a dead man.

THE EMBARRASSING
TRUTH ABOUT ME

"WHY CAN'T I FIGURE THIS out?"

I'm trying to build a barbecue grill for our campout in Joshua Tree National Park, but instead of a neat little barbecue, I'm stuck with a pile of parts that don't fit. It shouldn't be this hard.

I know the parts are supposed to make a folding propane grill to cook our burgers, but I can't figure it out. As the sun sets on the massive rock formations and Joshua Trees, snowflakes settle on my pile of grill parts. It's going to be a cold night in the desert.

I take a break from my barbecue and look up at storm clouds brewing above my head. Snowflakes meander softly down and settle on my forehead. I'd love to cook something for our camping group, but since I can't get the grill to work, cold and hunger are setting in...

Suddenly, the rock walls echo with the sounds of shouting. My friend Nathan is arguing with his wife. His graceful wife Stephanie whispers for him to keep his voice down. Nathan is one of my best friends on Earth. But he won't keep his voice down. He's frustrated. "Did you see Dave with that barbecue grill? He's as thick as a brick!"

This is embarrassing. Nathan is a dear friend who noticed something that not many people see. I'm not very smart; as he said, "Thick as a brick." Nathan is right. You need only watch me fumble with a simple task to know that my success in life is not due to any special ability on my part.

My life story is the road less traveled. I found myself on a unique path, not because I have a plan, but because of mistakes and poor planning. Time and again, I stumble forward as smart people like Nathan scratch their heads. Nathan is frustrated by my inability to grasp obvious things, but I'm very blessed to have a friend like Nathan who vents but then patiently helps me put the grill together before the storm hits.

When I succeed against odds, it's not because there's anything great about me. It's because I'm helped by friends like Nathan who are willing to pitch in. But there's something else. I've had help from someone I can't see. Someone up there has been guiding me, protecting me, and sometimes talking to me. Others have noticed it too.

GIBBS

O NE DAY, I OPEN THE door of a helicopter and find a movie pilot named David Gibbs. He seems like a nice guy, but there's something different about him. He has a lot of flair for a helicopter pilot...and poetry.

When pilots call the control tower, they speak in a methodical drone. "November Two Hotel Alpha, with information Yankee, for an East Transition." But Gibbs announces himself romantically, "Tower, good afternoon. I want to enter your sky." In all my years I've never heard anyone speak to FAA officials that way.

Gibbs is a unique person to "enter the sky" with. Of all the

Hollywood movie pilots, Gibbs is the only one who comes to work early and spends hours helping me build the camera. After the flight, when other pilots are already back at home, Gibbs stays into the wee hours of the night helping me remove the camera. He helps me carefully box up the delicate gyro-stabilized parts, and then he drives with me to the camera house to help me lift the heavy equipment back on the shelf.

As I get to know Gibbs, I discover that he's the most ambitious and driven person I've ever met. And he's kind-hearted. He acts like the big brother I never had. But, like a big brother, he picks on me relentlessly.

When Gibbs and I are flying for *The Amazing Race*, he doesn't call me by name, just "Peanut Head." So I correct him, "It's Mr. Peanut Head to you." And with that, we picked on each other every day since.

I explain that since we're both named Dave, it's confusing to the director of *The Amazing Race*. So we should have a system to know who's being addressed. For example, I can be Dave Number One and he can be Dave Number Two.

This makes perfect sense. But Gibbs, he doesn't get it. He says, "Negative, Peanut Head." He points to himself and speaks as if quoting Shakespeare, "I am an artist. The sky is my canvas. This helicopter is my paintbrush. And you are my little spittoon-boy."

That's ridiculous. I don't know what a spittoon-boy is.

I explain to Gibbs that in movies, cameramen are listed at the top of the credits and drivers like him are listed at the bottom — clearly in order of importance. Gibbs is like a glorified cabdriver, and his job is to drive me where I want to go. But he's never understood it. I know I'm right, but for some reason, we've argued about it every single day for 18 years. It's the funniest working relationship I've ever known.

One day a director points to me and says, "You're in charge." Finally, a proper hierarchy is established! I am undeniably Dave Number One. But Gibbs doesn't get it. He says I'm not in charge of anything, and my status is equivalent to foodservice workers that cook and clean for the crew.

> **"You sit in your little seat and point that camera where I tell you..."**
>
> **— David Gibbs**

Gibbs has such a driven personality I made a special ringtone for him. I know when Gibbs is calling because my phone announces him with the theme song for *Mission Impossible*.

One day I call Gibbs and discover he's in the next room, because his phone makes the sound of a flock of chickens singing the theme song from *Mission Impossible*. His custom ringtone for me is a chorus of chickens trying to sound like an action movie.

I know he knows when I'm calling, because his phone announces me with chickens. But he never says, "Hello, Dave," like a normal person. He picks up the phone and shouts, "Monkey!" or "Peanut!" How rude.

"Pan left, tilt down. OK. Hold on the sun." Gibbs tells me

exactly where to point the camera. I push the joystick on the Cineflex laptop controller. Electrons surge through advanced aerospace circuitry, and the Cineflex turns our pulsing, vibrating aircraft into a godlike perspective, perfectly floating above Los Angeles. Following Gibbs' cue, I find the sun poetically resting on the horizon.

As our helicopter weaves through the air, the gyro-stabilized Cineflex gimbal holds the telescopic lens so still that I can see sun spots, ninety-three million miles away. It is awe-inspiring, which could explain why the director is speechless in the front seat next to Gibbs.

Technically, the director is supposed to tell us what to do. But he sits, absolutely quiet, as we careen a thousand feet in the air, pulling G's and holding steady shots of objects in space. Right on Gibbs' cue, I tilt the camera down to find the human world below our skids.

Like an orchestral conductor, Gibbs counts me in. "OK. Three-two-one, now pull."

I pull, or zoom the camera lens away from the sun, to find a perfect silhouette of the Vincent Thomas Bridge, where the hero of the show drives between suspension towers.

The car and bridge are just steel and asphalt, but Gibbs paints them as an artist would use a paintbrush on canvas. Gibbs paints the bridge cables poetically across the camera image, as ships in the harbor a mile away lyrically rotate in my camera frame. The camera image is only two dimensional, but Gibbs steers us so that the moving picture has a lyrical depth.

I can see cars on the bridge, because my camera is looking through a gyro-stabilized telescope, but Gibbs is looking out the window with his naked eye and can somehow see which car has the hero. "OK. It's the third car, passing the stanchion....now!" Right on his cue, I find the car, perfectly framed, and you can see the star of the show in the driver's window, because while all this was happening, Gibbs was lowering the helicopter to car-height—exactly where we need to be to see the host of the show driving across the bridge.

But I have to let him know he was wrong about one thing.

"Number Two!" I shout. "That's not a stanchion. It's a tower."

"Negative, Peanut Brain! That's a stanchion. A stanchion is the thing that holds the bridge up."

I know there's a God, because He sent me to correct Gibbs.

"There's no such thing as a stanchion." I patiently remind him.

The director is sitting in the front seat of the helicopter next to Gibbs, watching the car drive across the bridge on his monitor. So I ask him to tell Gibbs that he's wrong. But the director says nothing; he just laughs. Dave and I have been arguing this way since we got up this morning.

All joking aside, Gibbs is great at what he does. I never told him, but he really is an artist. He cares so passionately about his "canvas" that I've spent much of my career simply pointing the camera where he says to. His skill and work ethic are a secret to my success. Gibbs has opened doors for me as a cameraman, hiring me on hundreds of TV shows. I couldn't ask for a more generous colleague or a better friend.

WALK AWAY

R EMEMBER NATHAN FROM THE BBQ story? The day I met Nathan, I knew he was smarter than me. I knew he would someday rise above me. I could have tried to keep him down and preserve my place over him, but, I'd rather teach him everything I know and help him grow. That's not very smart, but I've never been particularly smart about my career. In a quarter century of flying cameras, I've never once tried to hold anyone back from their potential, even if they end up taking my job.

I was right about Nathan. Within three years of training him, he became my boss at Wescam.

I think it's good that I treated him kindly. Now the boss is also a great friend, who remembers I treated him kindly when I didn't have to.

Now that he's the big boss, Nathan hunts through the Wescam building at the end of the day. He finds me up to my elbows in a complicated project. "So? What are you doing?" he asks.

But Nathan knows me well. He knows I'm going to work all night. I love my job so much I'll still be here when he comes into the office tomorrow morning. I'll be wearing the same clothes, and I'll still be up to my elbows in work.

"I'm going to clean this gimbal and straighten up the shop," I say, as if it's something anyone would do, all night long.

"No you're not. Go home," says Nathan. Like shooing a stray cat, he herds me out the door and into the parking lot. He points to my car and locks the office door so I can't come back until tomorrow. This is a strange situation. My boss told me to quit working, and then he *threw me out* of the building. But Nathan is a good friend,

43

and I suppose he's right about me. I should have more in my life than just work. But I love my work, which is why nothing could have prepared me or Nathan for what happens next...

As I'm walking through my house, I hear a voice, but there's no one here. It's just me in the house. The voice sounds familiar. It's the same voice that told me to put my mom and grandma on the phone, even though my mom was unable to speak. This time, the voice says something that takes my breath away. My head is spinning, and I can't believe what I'm told. It's un-thinkable. The sun sets outside my windows. Darkness falls around me, but I don't move a muscle. I'm just sitting in an empty house with the words playing over and over in my head.

The next day, I walk into Nathan's office at Wescam and plop down on a chair. Nathan looks up from his big-boss paperwork. He flashes a thoughtful smile. Nathan is very perceptive and, right away, he knows something's up.

"Well, good sir. How are you?" he asks.

I try to think how I can ease him into what I'm about to say, but I don't understand it.

"I quit."

Nathan is so smart he usually knows what I'm going to say before I say it. But, now his eyes grow wide, and he stares at me for a moment, speechless. Nothing could've prepared him for my resignation, as my career is sky-rocketing.

I've become quite well-known as the kind of company man who will memorize equipment manuals and stay up all night sweeping the floor. Nathan routinely has to order me to go home instead of working all night. No one loves their work more than I. But in the middle of a meteoric career, I suddenly give Nathan my two weeks' notice.

Nathan thinks for a minute and begins a bizarre negotiation where he offers to cut my hours and increase my pay, and I say, "No, thank you."

He stares at me in disbelief. I suppose that when smart people want a raise or promotion, they threaten to quit. But I'm not smart. This is not a game. I don't have a strategy.

I tell Nathan the truth. "I love my job. I love the people I work with. I don't want more money or less work. I'm not quitting because of hours or pay." Nathan looks like he's seen a ghost. Everyone I know at Wescam is shocked. My career couldn't be more rewarding or successful. But I heard a voice, and that familiar voice said something that changed my life. "Walk away." It sounds strange to me. I can't imagine life without my job. I don't know what I'll do without my dream of flying. But now it's real. I said the words.

But the more I think about quitting, the more I'm starting to like the idea—just like putting a phone to my comatose mother's ear. It's hard to explain, but it's starting to feel like a good idea. The voice tells me to quit my amazing career and spend more time with my loved ones.

So I resign from Wescam and immediately begin taking steps to sell my house. I have to sell my house, because without a job and paychecks, I can't keep a home and mortgage payments.

Of all the seven billion humans on Earth, I'm the one who gets to float between skyscrapers as the host of *Amazing Race* shouts, "Go!" into my camera. I have the privilege of steering a camera through the snow-covered mountains for the Winter Olympics. I'm floating above James Bond as he saves the world from super-villains. I get to soar across the sky over the Super Bowl as a hundred million people watch the game through my gyro-stabilized lens.

But I am turning away from all of that. I walk away from the fairytale opportunity that Ed Silva gave me when he opened the door to a clueless kid who wandered in off the street and started sweeping the floor. In an instant, I make the ludicrous choice to turn my life on a dime. I quit my dream job and "walk away" from the world of work and paychecks.

I honestly don't understand this chapter of my life. I have every reason not to do this. But I'm leaving my illuminated path to greatness and turning straight into the darkness of an uncertain future. I follow the voice and walk away from the thing that makes me perfectly happy—my career.

As the sun rises on my home, the air is filled with the sound of neighbors hurrying to work. By 9:10 am, all is quiet. The street's empty. Everyone's gone to work. I used to be right beside them, jamming into rush hour traffic to join the rat race. But not today. Today, I have nowhere to go and nothing to do. This is weird.

But, suddenly, the quiet of my jobless life is shattered by the sound of a telephone that rings with sad news. My grandma in Florida had a stroke and is near death. So I immediately buy a plane ticket to Florida. I would say I dropped everything to jump on the plane, but since I'd already quit my job, there was nothing to drop. So I go straight to Florida to help grandma.

As I pull the rental car into the hospital parking lot, I wonder how I'll pay for rental cars in the future without a job or income. I have no idea.

But I think of how hard it would be to take time away from my job at Wescam to visit my grandma. When I worked at Wescam, this trip would have been impossible. There's no way I could have left work to help grandma. I probably wouldn't have even gotten the message that she's sick for a while. I was traveling the world on a busy schedule, and I was unreachable most of the time.

But I quit my job. And I answered the call that brought me to grandma's side. Now, I take a deep breath and walk into the ICU, prepared for the worst. I've been warned that grandma's very close to death. I worry as I make my way past ventilator machines and the sickest of the sick. I don't know what I'm about to see.

Nurses and doctors in this ward are hyper-alert because patients like my grandma are on the brink of death. Plastic tubes pass fluid and air into their bodies. Without this artificial help, they would die in minutes. Some of them will die anyway. For others, it could go either way.

When they tell my grandma I'm in the room, she lights up, but not like a person. Her tear-filled eyes illuminate as bright as the sun.

I've never seen anything like it. My weary grandma smiles through medical tubes and needles. Her heart monitor bounces loudly, counting beats-per-minute as her heart races. She squeezes my hand as tears run down her tired features and onto hospital sheets.

She looks like she's seen a ghost...

My all-consuming career would never have allowed me to visit her. And she knows it as she lays in that bed, intubated, in pain, and staring at death all day long. When I arrive and stay by her side for two weeks, it means the world to her.

This hospital is full of every kind of life-saving equipment, but the thing that brings my grandma back to life is the miracle of a loved one who can't possibly be here. Miraculously, she's out of ICU in 24 hours. I've never seen a more complete turn-around in a sick human being.

I still don't understand the scene in *Star Wars* where Luke hears a voice and turns off his target computer. If he misses, the world will end. It makes no sense. But maybe letting go of your perfect aim allows you to hit a target for someone else. Maybe holding someone's hand can save the world, too.

I gave up my dream job. But somehow, without a job or money, I feel richer. And as my grandma walks and talks and laughs, it feels like success.

CAN WE HIRE YOU?

NATHAN IS CALLING FROM WESCAM. "I know you don't work for us anymore, but can we pay you to do a job for one day?"

"Sure." I say. And just like that, I'm a freelance photographer. That was fifteen years ago. And I've been working odd jobs for Wescam, and other companies, ever since.

I make less money. I don't get paychecks like I used to. But my life is richer.

BEWARE OF DOG

WHEN I'M HOME, WE DON'T talk about flying cameras, or cheating death. We talk about the little things. We don't talk about helicopters. We talk about kids and sports and, sometimes, family pets.

"This dog needs a home." My friend points to his dog. It's an adorable golden lab. I love dogs, but I'm even less able to care for a dog than my friend who has to get rid of the dog because his family has lost interest.

"We just don't have time for the dog," says my friend, hinting that he wants me to take him and give him a home. I'm a little heart-broken. I wish I could take the dog and give him a good home, but I can't. I'm not home enough. The dog couldn't survive at my house. He'd poop and pee on everything, and then he'd starve to death.

So I turn down the offer to adopt my friend's dog, and that's the end of it, until one night when I see a little black dog running in traffic. The stray dog has a collar and tag, so I know it has a home and has probably just gotten lost. I love dogs and think about how much it would mean to the owner to have the lost dog back in one piece.

A car slides sideways as the driver swerves to avoid the hapless dog. Big offroad tires skip as the driver of a pickup truck slams on his brakes, but he can't stop. The giant pickup truck goes right over the dog, who's frozen in fear. The little dog doesn't understand what's happening. It just stands, frozen in fear, as the truck passes overhead. Various cars swerve and screech to a halt as they encounter the dog in their lanes.

A black dog on black pavement is hard for drivers to see at night. The dog is going to get killed by a car any second. The dog stares blankly at the cars, weaving and sliding to avoid hitting it. People are honking their horns, but the dog doesn't know what car horns are. The little dog is scared and is just standing in the road, wandering a little, left and right, as cars and trucks swirl over the dog's head.

So I stop my car and walk into traffic to save the dog. But when the dog sees me, she bolts and runs into a gas station. Now she's hiding under a car. Nuts. What am I doing in traffic? This crazy dog doesn't even want to be saved. I wave at drivers who are now in danger of running into *me* standing in the middle of the road. I scramble off the street.

People walk out of the gas station, and the little dog wiggles out from under the car and charges them, growling and snarling. The people run in fear. Wow! That's a mean little dog!

I call a friend of mine who's an animal expert. I tell him I'm trying to help this stray dog, and he comes down to help. He puts on heavy gloves and reaches to drag the vicious dog out from under the car. The dog reacts like a Tasmanian Devil, snarling and biting. My friend has to let go. The little dog wiggles back under the car. Stalemate.

We decide to ask the car's owner to let us push the car away from the dog with the engine off, so as not to kill the dog when they drive away. We carefully push the car to reveal a little black dog covered in motor oil.

This dog didn't just get lost; she appears abused and neglected. She has no hair on her back, just scarred, bare skin covered in scabs. She's thirsty, starving to death, and covered in motor oil. The tag I thought I saw is really just a part of the choke-chain that's grown tight around her neck. "That dog has been running in traffic all day," says a neighbor. Poor animal.

No one's cared enough to try to rescue the vicious little beast.

But now the angry dog is exposed and seems to not know what to do. My friend gets on the phone and tries to get animal control to come capture it. The streets of Los Angeles are busy tonight, and animal control isn't answering the phone. So as my friend sits on hold, I take a careful look at the mutt.

I don't want the dog to be sent to the pound, but this dog is vicious and won't let us get near. I don't know what else to do, except to get professional animal control on the case.

This dog is going to bite someone and get hit by a car tonight...

But animal control still doesn't answer, so it's up to me. The only thing I can think of is to offer food and water. I carefully pour some food into a dish and slide it towards the furry monster. The dog inhales the food. She's starving to death. I pour some water into the dish. "Here you go." I talk to the dog as if I've always known her. She eyes me warily, but licks the bowl dry. And now she lets me sit...a little bit closer...

"It's okay, sweetheart." I say to the fur-dragon. I carefully wiggle closer to the beast. Her vicious body language eases up a bit and she lies down next to the water bowl I gave her. Now I can feel that the dog is relaxing, and she seems to accept me in her space. It's been two hours since I got out of my car.

"Okay. I got them! Animal control will come and get her!" My friend is excited and sounds relieved. He finally has animal control on the phone. I look at the vicious dog who's now just a few feet away. I know animal control officers will euthanize her tonight.

With thousands of dogs running loose on the streets of South Central LA, they're not going to waste time with an aggressive dog. They'll lasso her like a crocodile and drag her by the neck to a waiting poison needle. She'll be euthanized and die alone in a cage...

It's no big deal, just a wild stray dog, abused and neglected. There's no way to save this unfortunate beast. Obviously, no one cares for the hostile mutt. She outgrew her choker chain weeks ago, and no one bothered to remove it before throwing her out on the street. Now it squeezes her in a strangle hold because she continued to grow, and now her neck is bigger than the chain.

There's no conceivable happy ending here, but as I look down at the dog who's been snarling and biting, something comes over me. A voice tells me I have to do something unthinkable. An overwhelming sense of unreasonable purpose fills my being, just like when I quit my job.

"Tell them not to come." I say with absolute certainty.

"What?!" My friend is dumbfounded. He stares at me in disbelief for a moment, then covers the phone so animal control can't hear my ridiculous plan.

"Really?" he reasons. "They'll come out. You don't want them to come?"

"They're just going to kill her," I say. "Tell them not to come."

"OK." He pauses, takes a deep breath and puts the phone back to his ear. "Never mind. You don't have to come. We'll take care of it."

Considering my friend tried diligently for an hour to get animal control on the phone, I'm sure he didn't expect to hang up on them. He puts the phone away and stares at me. Now what?

I have no idea "now what?" There's a vicious, biting beast a few feet away, and I just refused help from the only people equipped to handle it. I don't know how to do this, but I have to. So I move closer. I'm pretty sure the dog is going to bite me.

Now we sit side-by-side. I stare at the dog, who's wary, but relaxing more as time goes by. I do nothing. I just sit and wait. An hour passes. Over time, I move an inch closer to claws and teeth.

I take a borrowed leash and cautiously reach toward the beast. But the dog doesn't bite. She doesn't even react, although she sees my hand approaching her neck. Expecting the worst, I grab the dog's chain and click the leash on it.

My breath is taken by what happens next. Nothing. The attack dog doesn't attack. She doesn't growl or bite. She acts as if I always put a leash on her when it's time to leave.

So I stand up and leave the gas station. She stands up and walks right beside me all the way to my car. It looks like the vicious dog and I have been to obedience class a hundred times.

I stop by my car door, and the dog stops and sits down. She looks up at me as if she's known me all her life, and her only purpose is to go wherever I go.

"What are we going to do now?" my friend asks with trepidation.

"I'm going to take her home."

"How are you going to get her in the car?" he gasps.

"I'm going to pick her up and put her on the seat."

"You are?" My friend is right. This is unthinkable. The dog is a monster. I think there'll be blood, but I don't know what else to do. I have to get the dog to safety, and that means she has to go with me. Although I'm about to be mauled, I feel a strange mixture of excitement and peace. I reach down, pick up the vicious dog and put her in the car, as if that's what we always do. The dog doesn't bite. She calmly sits and, I believe, breathes a sigh of relief. I can relate. Sometimes when I don't fit in with the "normal" crowd, it feels good to belong. It feels good to be loved despite my flaws.

We drive the vicious dog to my place and wash the motor oil off of her. What we find under the dirt and grease is shocking — the most affectionate dog I've ever met.

How can this be? She charged everyone who got near and bit them. My friend was bitten. But after three hours of patient work, I clicked the leash on the beast and, in that moment, she became my best friend. She doesn't look at me like a normal dog. She looks at me as if she'd chew through a burning building to save me.

But I can't keep a dog. I'm now a freelance cameraman. I travel the world for work. I'm not home enough to care for a dog. And I certainly can't risk keeping a vicious dog who bites everyone who approaches. I can't see a way out of this situation. There's no reasonable path forward.

But once again, something comes over me. And this time, I know what it is. That dog is just like me. We're both flawed. We both need help. If I deserve help from above, then this dog deserves help from me. I have no idea how I'm going to make this work, but I'll do it.

I take the dog to a vet. After she growls at everyone in the animal hospital, the vet patiently examines her, noting fierce aggression and...hip dysplasia.

"Hip dysplasia?"

The vet explains that she was born with bad hips. There's no help and no cure for it.

She'll never outgrow this problem. Her body is flawed and will only get worse, ending in painful, debilitating arthritis. She'll end up crippled by the hips God gave her.

I have no idea how to take care of a dog with bad hips, especially one who bites.

I decide to name her Switch, because she switched from vicious attack to protective love.

The next day I have to go to the airport and build a camera to fly over Los Angeles. Gibbs and I work more than twelve hours at a time. I can't come home to feed the dog or let her out to pee. So I put her in my car, and Switch, the lame biting dog, goes with me to the airport.

In between helicopter flights, I put on a leash and take her for a walk. I have food for her in the truck, and I pour water bottles into a bowl. It's a funny, homeless sort of life, but it works. I have no plan other than minute-by-minute, day-by day, what I need to do to take care of the vicious dog.

I worry about her because, although I leave the windows open for her while I'm out flying, I can't leave them open all the way because she'll bite a passerby. And on hot days, there's a danger of heat in the car.

So I decide to do something crazy. I start shopping for a mobile home for the dog. That way she can live comfortably, without the danger of heat exhaustion in my car while I'm out flying over Los Angeles with Gibbs.

I'm pretty sure the RV dealer had never had a customer like me. My little car can't pull Switch's trailer, so I have to buy a giant pickup truck to pull the RV trailer. Now Switch can travel with me to jobs in air-conditioned comfort. I know what you're thinking. This is nuts.

It's strange, but it's also kind of fun. I drive Switch and the RV to the Super Bowl, where Gibbs and I are flying for FOX Network. We shoot the stadium for the biggest game of the year and, at the end of the day, when people are going to bars and Super Bowl parties, Gibbs and I land and tie nylon straps over the helicopter blades. Gibbs heads to a hotel, and I walk a few feet from the aircraft to the RV, and I'm home with Switch. I feed her and walk her, and I lift her up into the camper bed.

Switch is the most faithful kind of friend. The only thing she cares about is being by my side. At night I look at the vicious beast sleeping next to me. I don't know how we'll get through tomorrow, but we got through today, and that's enough.

I don't know how I'm going to make this work. I have no plan to care for the vicious, crippled dog, just a willingness to do whatever it takes.

Don't jump in my truck when I'm not there. You might lose a body part.

Where we'll go, and how we'll make this work tomorrow, I have no idea. In spite of the expense and inconvenience, I feel that, in some way, my life is richer. And I am blessed.

Because I've never owned an aggressive dog, I spend hours reading books about vicious dogs. I study and practice the steps to safely keep a dog that bites. It's a lot of work.

Switch doesn't train easily. I walk her every day, but she resists training. In fact, it takes a year of patient work to teach her to walk on a leash. I'm not surprised she was abused and thrown in the street. Most people wouldn't take the time to do all of this.

I never have to tell Switch what to do. She just knows. If she escapes the house, she never leaves, just sits by my door and waits for me to let her back in. She'll wait there all day and night. She doesn't want to go anywhere else, doesn't want to be with anyone else.

You know how dogs bark at every little sound? Not Switch. She NEVER barks unless someone is coming.

Some dogs bark at intruders but run and hide if someone breaks into the house and the owners aren't around. So I decide to sneak around the house to see how Switch will handle an intruder.

I've tried this with other dogs. When I snuck up on my ex-girlfriend's dog, the dog barked at me, then peed on the floor and ran away.

So I sneak to the front door and pounce out of the bushes. I'm not wearing normal clothing, but a dark hooded disguise. But Switch doesn't pee and flee. She charges to the end of her rope like a heat-seeking missile. It looks like she's being shot out of a cannon in an explosion of claws and teeth. Reaching the end of her rope, Switch then tries to pull the house off its foundation so she can get close enough to bite me.

When she realizes it's not an intruder but me in a hoodie disguise, she has a happiness explosion and greets me with intense love. She wags her tail with all her might and runs in circles, as if her heart will pound out of her chest.

That's how I learned that if a threat comes to the house, Switch won't back down. She'll defend me with her life.

A friend points out that when we're in the house, Switch always faces the door, like a furry gargoyle.

"Look at how she puts herself between you and the door," my friend says.

"Oh. I never noticed that."

"Pay attention. She's guarding you."

My friend is right. Switch has been guarding me for eleven years. I don't know if I rescued Switch, or Switch rescued me. We've come a long way since we found each other.

I put my boots on many times a day, but somehow Switch always knows when I'm just going outside to walk around the house, and when I'm going to get in the truck and drive away. That's when she runs in between me and the door. She can't talk, but she knows how to make it clear that she doesn't want me to leave, unless I'm going to put her in the truck and take her with me. And that's exactly what I do. I take Switch everywhere I go.

"How did you end up with such a vicious dog?" my neighbor Suzee asks. I explain how I found Switch on the streets of Los Angeles, and that it's a herculean task to manage an aggressive dog. For some reason it brings a tear to my eye when I tell the story of Switch and me.

I've taken Switch with me for eleven years now. Everywhere we go is a ridiculous challenge. It's a lot of work. If you meet Switch, I'll ask you not to pet her because she still bites. But after eleven years, I can honestly say that this crazy dog is the most loyal friend and protector I have on Planet Earth. I'm glad she's here.

GRAVITY

THERE ARE A HANDFUL OF people on Earth who ride a helicopter with a movie camera. One of them owns a company in Europe. He's a fun-loving, friendly man who always goes out of his way to say hello when he sees me in the helicopter hangar. He lights the room up with his cheerful smile. So I'm shocked to learn that we lost him in a helicopter crash. How can somebody so full of life be dead? But unfortunately his pilot made a mistake, and their helicopter fell out of the sky in what is known as a "death spiral."

Gravity doesn't forgive mistakes. Gravity doesn't care if you're a nice person. Gravity's a relentless bitch who took my colleague's life.

No one can save you from bad choices and gravity. I know, because right now gravity has me. Like my deceased colleague, I'm sitting in a helicopter that's falling out of the sky. I try to pull myself vertical as the aircraft tumbles over backwards. I try to look down at the city below, but the world is a blurry ground-rush avalanche.

Our downfall is brought by pilot error. But my pilot isn't through. He makes another mistake that causes us to spin violently as we fall out of the sky in a picture-perfect death spiral. We're doomed. My European colleague entered this state of flight, and he was never seen again. We lost his warm smile and laughter in a violent downward spiral just like this one. They call it a "Death Spiral" for good reason. My vision is blurred as we spin to the ground. I can barely make out the buildings below, which are coming up to meet us like an upper-cut punch. This is going to hurt.

I cling to my headset, which is being ripped off my head by the G-forces. I look up at the pilot and find him staring straight ahead as the buildings spin closer and closer to us.

But I know that there are guardian angels because, just before impact, the helicopter magically starts flying again. My pilot is flailing on the controls. He made deadly mistakes. But our death spiral ends, and the unforgiving laws of physics relax for a moment to let us back into the sky. Not a word is spoken as we magically climb back to safe altitude and fly back to base.

I'll never fly with this pilot again. I'm lucky to be alive. But is it luck that saved me? Some of my colleagues have done the very same death spiral, and they're dead.

So ends another day at the office. It's one of a thousand days that no one knows about. I've never told a soul what I do at work, or what it looks like when things go wrong.

NEW ORLEANS

"**D**O YOU WANT TO GO to New Orleans?"

The President of Helinet Aviation is on the phone. Helinet has news helicopter crews all over the country. The owner, Alan Purwin, is the renowned Hollywood movie pilot from my NASA story, but Alan is not *just* a movie pilot. He's also an entrepreneur and visionary.

Right now Alan is on an adventure, flying one of his news helicopters into New Orleans, which has been abandoned to hurricane floodwaters. Alan made the bold decision to fly alongside the Coast Guard helicopters that swooped into the flooded city to rescue stranded victims. And now Alan wants a cameraman to go to New Orleans.

I'm sure he has at least fifty news cameramen on staff who'd love an opportunity to cover the biggest story of our lifetime. Right now a major American city sits empty, with flood water over the roofs.

But I'm not a live-news cameraman. So I ask him why he picked me. "Don't you have guys who want to go?"

"It's rough down there," says the Helinet president. "There are no hotels. I don't know where you'll sleep."

What? There's no plan? We don't know how it will work, or where I'll sleep? Of course I say yes, and they put me on the next flight to New Orleans.

On the plane ride I wonder what New Orleans will be like after the apocalypse of Hurricane Katrina. On arrival, I find our helicopter in an unusual situation. N1231A is surrounded by giant military C130 Hercules, CH47 Chinooks, and H-60 Blackhawks. It looks like a science fiction movie.

Alan Purwin lands in the middle of the streets of the ruined city. People no longer drive cars in New Orleans. Our helicopter is the only vehicle on a road built to carry millions of cars.

There are no other news helicopters in the sky above New Orleans. When Alan Purwin flew in with first responders, he was granted exclusive access to fly a news camera over the drowning city. Every picture that goes to the outside world comes from his helicopter and Cineflex camera.

The city is ruined; there's no electricity and no way to get around on the ground to see the whole story. News vans can't get in or out. Most Americans see New Orleans through Alan's lens, because all news agencies are pulling from the only live camera that can go anywhere in the flooded city. We fly alone above the disturbing sight of an entire city, completely ruined and shut down. If you've seen the movie *I am Legend*, you have some idea of the scene below our skids.

We land for fuel in the middle of Interstate 10. Alan parks his helicopter next to his satellite truck. The operator in the satellite truck points to a half-dozen TV screens. "Our pictures are live on Fox, CNN, ABC, CBS, NBC." I've never seen anything like it. Every network is showing our airborne pictures of the sunken city.

Cameraman and LAPD Reservist JT Alpaugh has been flying over the flooded city for a week with Helinet owner and movie pilot Alan Purwin.

They say I will relieve JT from his camera job, so he can help Alan to watch out for other helicopters. That makes no sense. I've flown in helicopters around the world and have never seen a situation where the pilot can't see where he's going.

But I learn that things are different in New Orleans after the storm.

As we fly over New Orleans, military helicopters pick people up from flooded neighborhoods and take them to dry ground at the Super Dome and a freeway interchange.

If you were told that the Federal Government didn't help victims of Hurricane Katrina, I'm afraid you've been given fake news. I personally witnessed Air Force, Navy, Army, and Coast Guard crews rescuing thousands from their flooded homes. The military pilots have strict rules when flying over civilian cities, but they had to set those rules aside in a mad-dash effort to save people from their drowning homes.

Military helicopters fly in every direction. It looks like that scene in *Star Wars* where the fighters swarm above the Death Star. These military helicopters are so fast, and so many, it's like flying through a hornet's nest. We're in constant danger of crashing into them. That's why JT had to quit filming and climb into the front with Alan to help navigate.

As we fly through the unbelievable sights of a submerged city, JT reports live to network audiences while pointing and gesturing for me to pan, tilt, and zoom in to what he's talking about.

We take off from the improvised military base at Baton Rouge Airport and fly over a surreal landscape of water and mud with buildings in between. The giant city is a ghost town, with water halfway up the telephone poles. Cars are underwater. Nothing moves on the streets except small boats.

Alan sets down in the middle of Interstate 10 to refuel and coordinate with the TV networks. It feels weird to stand motionless on a freeway where thousands of cars normally travel at high speed. I expect to get hit by a car, but nothing moves except our helicopter. We have the entire freeway to ourselves.

Our satellite truck camps on Interstate 10 and feeds every network. The news networks have our pictures onscreen around the clock as the levees leak and flood waters pour into New Orleans' homes.

There're no cars moving, no ambulances, no police. When Alan takes off, he pulls the trigger on his Aerospatiale stick and talks on the radio to military air traffic controllers who've taken control of the New Orleans sky. Alan is joined by the voices of C-130 and Blackhawk pilots flying rescue missions.

High rise buildings have holes punched in them by hurricane winds. The storm ripped the roof off the Super Dome.

That's when we see him, a man walking in waist-deep mud to get to his sunken house. Alan pulls into a hover and radios the military AWACS to call in a rescue for the stranded man. A giant military helicopter thunders up beside us and lowers a lifeline to the man.

JT reports live to the networks as the military helicopter crew works to save him.

But the man refuses. He doesn't want to be rescued. I can't contain myself. "What?! You've got to be kidding me!" I gasp.

Alan and JT frantically wave at me to shut up. Every news network in America has our camera on-the-air, and they can hear my voice.

I feel bad for ruining the moment. I'm not a very good news cameraman. Witnessing this surreal moment of apocalyptic human craziness, I forgot to filter myself and said, out loud, what I was thinking.

I'm flabbergasted. This poor flood-soaked man has two helicopters hovering over his head offering him a way out of the ruined neighborhood. Inside his home the sewage mixed with storm water stinks in the New Orleans heat. He's stranded. This man can't talk to anyone outside of his abandoned neighborhood. There's no internet, no cell service, and nothing to eat or drink.

But the helmeted military crewman shakes his head at us and waves to indicate that the man refuses to leave his ruined neighborhood. That poor man has lost everything and has two helicopters ready to lift him to safety, but he refuses to leave his flooded home. I don't get it.

THE GIFT

"DON'T SHIT WHERE YOU EAT," a friend of mine shares his colorful advice against dating at work. I always take his advice, but I made an exception to date a producer who's supervising me on a TV show. The show was short-lived, but I continue to date her for two years after the show ends. It's a great time in my life.

One day, as I'm working on the yard at the girlfriend's house, she storms up to me with a look on her face that suggests someone just died. But what she says is amazing. She's pregnant. How can that be? She takes birth control pills religiously.

She's panic-stricken and says, "This is not our only option." She's referring to giving birth in the age of abortion. But it *is* my only option. I can't be a part of abortion, killing an innocent life, especially one that beat the 99% odds written on the back of her birth control pills. So I tell her we can handle this. I love kids. I love life.

The bottom line is I don't have a clear, well-thought-out plan for things. I know I stumbled my way into this situation. Raising kids is difficult. But, at this point in my life, I have to do the right thing, even if I don't know how I'll do it.

I'm planning to spend my life with the girlfriend, but I wait until we're on a family trip to one of her favorite places to propose. We're on a beautiful cliff next to a lighthouse when I get down on one knee. I want her to feel special, and that I'm not just doing it because she's pregnant. She says yes, and we're engaged.

MEAN STREETS

THE FIANCÉ AND I HAVE tried for a year to buy a house in the mean streets of Los Angeles.

I bought a bicycle so I can explore the area she chose to live. But something goes wrong.

I'm peddling up and down the hills in the neighborhood when I see a little dog running in between cars in rush-hour traffic.

The cute little Chihuahua has a collar and a tag, so I know it belongs to someone who'll be relieved if I can save it from being hit by a car. Uh-oh. Here I go again...

Throwing caution to the wind, I lay my bike over and run between cars to save the little dog from certain death. I pick the dog up and carry him out of danger. The little dog trembles in my hands. I guess the screeching cars gave the little guy quite a scare.

Suddenly, a van screeches to a halt and a desperate man looks intently at the animal I'm holding.

What follows next is the shortest conversation of all time, as the man grabs his dog without even saying "Thank you," and he storms off to his van, which suddenly reminds me of a serial killer van. Nuts.

The dog rescue took two minutes, but when I turn to find my bike, there is no bike. The bike is gone. Some heartless criminal stole my bike while I was rescuing the little dog a few feet away. The thief must have watched me save the dog and stole my bicycle the instant my back was turned. Sometimes I hate this city.

With no bicycle, I walk back to the fiancé's house. I'll have to continue looking for a house on foot.

We search for a home in the city for over a year, but never find anything we like that can accommodate our growing family. Even crime-ridden shacks are ridiculously priced in LA. A decent home costs almost a million dollars.

For a time, it looks like we found a house. We're close to buying a mountaintop property on her street, but mysteriously the fiancé backs out mid-offer. That's a shame. Back to the drawing board and a two-inch stack of LA property listings.

HOUSE NOT FOR SALE

A S USUAL, I'M NOT BEING entirely reasonable.
I want a house on a big piece of land in LA, but real estate is insane. The homes I can afford are tiny, on a piece of land so small that you can reach out your window and touch your neighbor's window.

An expensive home in LA is like a cheap apartment anywhere else. You can hear your neighbors arguing and partying. Backyards in LA usually consist of a tiny piece of dirt bordered by your neighbor's walls.

Some homes have no yard at all, just pavement. Many homes are so small, people don't have a place to park their car. Every night after work they wander the city streets to find a parking spot, but the streets are already full of parked cars, because fifteen million people got off work at the same time, jammed the streets to a standstill, and then inched their way to a tiny house with no parking. So they drive around, park on another street, and walk back to their houses. And for this they spend so much money that the mortgage payment becomes an all-consuming burden. A typical mortgage for a tiny ramshackle house in LA would crush most humans.

One of the homes we found is a bombed-out crack-house. The doors are kicked in. There are jagged shards of glass in the rotting window sills. There's no grass in the tiny yard, which is paved over with busted concrete. Someone twisted razor wire around the back of the house in a feeble attempt to ward off marauding criminals who've broken in multiple times and spray-painted gang signs on walls. Nothing lives at this house except some rats.

71

The yard consists of weeds that are growing up through cracks in the concrete. It's a classic shit-hole, but the price is a half-million dollars — more than I can afford. Sometimes I hate LA.

We spend two years looking for a home in LA. Nothing. We can't find anything we like. And my affordable price range only allows a small, modest home, with no parking, and no room for my growing family. Then one day I see an ad for a big house on a sprawling lot. This property is in the mountains above LA. The property is so big it has its own forest of trees — unheard of in Los Angeles. It takes my breath away. The home is an enormous custom-made Craftsman-style home that looks like a mansion. Normally this would be a ten-million-dollar estate. But for some reason, they're asking half the price of the bombed-out crack-house we saw in the city. I take a deep breath and stare at the computer screen. "Either this isn't what it seems or it's the chance of a lifetime." I gasp.

I tell the fiancé it's time to look at a house in the mountains above the city. Her reaction could best be described as World War III. Her head explodes when I tell her about the big house in the mountains. I don't know why she's so angry. We looked at homes up there before, and she said the area is OK. So I take the RV camping in the mountains to look at the house and get some time away from her.

I contact a real estate agent in the mountains and tell him I want to look at the house I saw on the internet. He laughs. "Did you find this on the internet?" He pauses dramatically to chuckle at my foolishness. "That house is not for sale, Dave."

"Fine," I say. "I'm coming with my RV to camp in the forest and you can show me some houses that *are* for sale."

When I arrive at his office the next day, my agent seems shocked by unexpected news. "That house *is* for sale! I had to research it!" he says.

He drives me around the forested neighborhoods in the mountains and we look at his favorite listings. When he pulls into the driveway at the house I found on the internet, he slams on the brakes and stares in stunned disbelief at one of the nicest homes on the mountain. He searches the MLS listing document for typos. This can't be... "They're selling *this house* for *that price*?!!!" He stares at the magnificent home like he's seen a ghost.

He unlocks the front door and shows me around the most beautiful home I've ever seen. I can't believe that they're selling a dream home for less than the price of a crack-house. I know I have to act. I tell him I want to go back to his office and put an offer in right away, but he tries to talk me out of it. "Now hold on Dave. I wouldn't do that. This is a foreclosure. It's Friday afternoon. Banks don't do business on weekends. They'll just use your offer to bring higher offers. Then they won't even tell you when they sell it to someone else for more money." I listen to him, but something tells me not to listen. So I say, "Call the seller's agent."

My agent rolls his eyes a bit. I think he's had enough of my magical thinking. People like me don't get to own a house like this in LA. Reluctantly, he takes his phone out as if humoring a child. He dials the agent who listed the house for sale.

"Mmhmmm. Well, but...OK...Alright."

"What did he say?" I ask with the enthusiasm of a kid at Christmas.

My agent tries to throw a wet blanket to curb my enthusiasm, but he acts as if he can't believe his own words. "Ummm. He said that there are no offers on the property and we should put an offer in...today."

I'm immune to wet blankets.

"Let's go back to your office right now and put an offer in."

As we drive through the forest to get to my agent's office, I can't contain my excitement. I know that this is a once-in-a-lifetime opportunity. Now is the time. I think about the mansion and the ridiculous notion I could own it, and a strange feeling comes over me. I decide to do something crazy. When my agent hands me the real estate offer agreement, I take it...and I draw a line through every page. I scratch out every single clause that gives me a way out of the deal. I cross out the termite contingency, the leaky-roof contingency, the busted-plumbing, shoddy-electrical and nuclear waste contingency (yes there is one). I even cross out the "I was in a strange mood when I offered to buy the house and now I want my deposit back" contingency (yes, there's one of those too).

Instead of giving me every right to change my mind and get my deposit back, I sign a contract that says I'm buying the house no matter what. If the house collapses under its own weight because termites secretly ate all the wood, then I'm buying the pile of sawdust.

After putting the offer in, I drive back down to the city. The fiancé's reaction can best be described as World War IV. When her fit of rage is done, I stand in front of her. I know what I'm doing. She calms down and says, "You're not buying anything until I see it." So we jump in the car and drive up into the mountains. We get there after dark. The home doesn't have electricity, which means no lights. She steps out of the car and silently turns to see a vast sea of city lights.

She says nothing, just stares at the view. Even the driveway is breathtaking.

There's a tangible change in her foul mood. She walks into the house and peers through the empty darkness of the open floor plan at the custom mahogany counters and cabinets. Even in the dark, the house is spectacular. She walks across the sprawling hardwood floors, sits on a built-in bench, and says, "Well this is nice. And it's the only house that we both like. Besides, it's cheap enough that we can still buy a house in the city." Just like that, without seeing more than was illuminated by my pen-light, she decides that the dream house will be OK.

In spite of my agent's dubious warnings that "Banks don't sell houses on weekends!" he calls on Saturday morning and says, "Congratulations. You got the house." It took them less than 24 hours, and they're not going to wait for a bigger offer like he said. They didn't even wait until Monday. The bank jumped at my offer, on the spot, sight-unseen, no questions asked...I think there's a lesson there. You can undo a thousand pages of red tape if you make a bold statement about how hungry you are for what's being offered.

And that's how I came to own a mansion in the sky.

This was no accident. People like me don't get to buy big, beautiful homes like that. Something magic is happening. I can feel that I'm being helped and guided by an unseen force. The "House Not for Sale" was sold for a fraction of its value. It's a spectacular gift.

We open escrow, and I talk to one of our new neighbors. He says, "Dave, after you looked at the house, the place turned into Grand Central Station. We saw 40-50 people climbing all over your property (apparently my real estate agent warned me against buying the house so he could go back and try to get all his friends to buy instead). Corruption is the way of the world, I suppose. Little people like me usually get the scraps left over, but not this time. I got a dream home, hand-built by the founders of a tiny town called Sky Forest."

DIRTY DEAL

M Y REAL ESTATE AGENT PROVED that little people don't get big houses. He "lost" my deposit check. The bank accepted the offer, but my real estate agent didn't give them the money like he was supposed to. I'm devastated. He went to such lengths to show the home to other people, but failed to honor his responsibility to execute my deal. Disgusting.

Under ordinary circumstances the deal would fall apart, especially if the funds don't come through from my offer and my real estate agent is showing the house to all of his friends, who have cash ready.

But something unusual happens and the big, uncaring bank stands by my offer, although my agent didn't deliver the money.

I believe that there *is* magic in this world. I believe that there *is* more to life than dollars and cents. When my agent failed to pay the seller, I should have lost the house. But I didn't.

When he said, "That house is not for sale," maybe he was right. Maybe I made a wish and my wish came true. The bank hung in with me, and in spite of every reason not to, we got the keys to a dream home in the sky.

YOU TOLD ME ABOUT THIS BEFORE IT HAPPENED

Heaven's half-acre. Sky Forest is a magic place. Clouds form at the house out of thin air. We're in the Mojave Desert. But, our first winter we got more snow than Michigan.

I fly in the clouds for a living, but I've never seen a house in the clouds until now. We're five thousand feet above the asphalt jungle of downtown LA.

One day, a dear friend, Chris Castro, visits us on Cloud Nine and can hardly believe the surreal environment. Then he says something that takes my breath away. "You described this place to me ten years ago."

"I did?" How can that be? I've never even heard of a place like this, except in a surrealist painting.

But Chris reminds me of a conversation we had ten years ago, when we said where we each wanted to be in ten years. I said I dreamed of living on top of a mountain, outside the city. I said I wanted a big piece of land, surrounded by nature, where I could raise a family.

At the time, I had no kids and didn't even know there were homes in the mountains above Los Angeles. I'd never heard of Sky Forest. Cloud Nine is unimaginable in the graffiti and asphalt Chris and I were in ten years ago. But here I am, ten years later, exactly as I'd dreamed in every detail. My impossible wish came true.

Chris is right. I described my impossible happy place ten years ago. And then I magically got the keys to Cloud Nine. But, as usual, I didn't know what I was doing. I had no plan, just an unreasonable wish. Now I'm standing in the clouds, surrounded by Christmas trees covered in snow, looking at the dream home where my mail gets delivered.

FOREST OF THE SKY

THE PACIFIC AND NORTH AMERICAN continental plates are separated by a crack in the Earth known as the San Andreas Fault. For eleven million years, pressure between the continental plates at the San Andreas Fault has been pushing the earth up into the sky. Magically, the ground rose eleven thousand feet in the air, causing a Jack-and-the-Beanstalk effect, forming the tallest mountains in Southern California.

Ten thousand years before Christopher Columbus set foot in North America, Native Americans climbed out of the Mojave Desert and found a cloud forest full of life. They believed there's magic in the trees and animals here. They believed the mountain has a spirit. For ages they told mystical legends of the plants, animals, and people here.

In 1919, American settlers bought 440 acres a mile above Los Angeles. They paid $10,000 for the property and named it "Forest of the Sky." When they built the Post Office, they had to shorten the town name so it would fit on a postage stamp — Sky Forest.

The founders of Sky Forest built an amazing little town in the sky. Then they built a tourist attraction for children, Santa's Village.

For forty years, millions of city dwellers drove up to Santa's Village theme park — a magical realm where snow sometimes piles six feet high, and Christmas lives all year round.

The dry, sunny weather of L.A. attracted a crowd of eighteen million people and Hollywood movie makers. But it's also a barren desert. The grass is always greener on the other side, except for LA, where the desert heat keeps grass dead and brown most of the year. To get grass to grow in LA, you have to create an oasis and fill it with your garden hose.

But above the city in Sky Forest, clouds magically form and stick to the trees. This creates a cloud-forest phenomenon known as horizontal rain. Cloud moisture drips from the leaves and falls onto the roots of the forest. The grass grows lush and green without a sprinkler system in our yard. A technicolor green carpet sparkles with magical drip irrigation.

Ever since I drew my first breath in Sky Forest, I count every second I'm here. I love every inch of this mile-high mountain. Have you ever watched someone take a drag on a cigarette and close their eyes, savoring the sweet addiction? That's how I feel about the mountaintop home I call Cloud Nine. Moving to Cloud Nine was like walking into a surrealist dream.

October 28, 2009, our son Wyatt was born. We've lived happily-ever-after in our tiny city house and a magic castle in Sky Forest. We are blessed.

Considering how little money we have, this is an amazing life. You might assume I make big bucks because I work on TV shows, but ever since I gave up my salary career to do odd jobs, I have more love than money.

But I'm so happy. Life is good.

And on Cloud Nine, life is beautiful.

THE LAST WORD

"OK Peanut Head. Put my camera on that bridge."
I'm flying with Gibbs for MTV's *Real World,
New Orleans.* The building tops are drifting below
my feet as Gibbs paints his canvas. He pulls on the collective, and
we rise above the Superdome. The roof has been repaired since
Hurricane Katrina. The shiny dome falls through my Cineflex frame
like a poem in motion, revealing the Crescent City connection.
Gibbs has flown cameras so many times he automatically knows
where to put me and the camera to look at the most dazzling view
of the city and the bridge.

"Three, two, one, now pull." Gibbs counts me down.

I press the zoom lever on the Cineflex laptop and our gyro-
stabilized telescope reveals the rooftops, the roads, and three
hundred thousand people working, walking, and driving in the
Big Easy.

Gibbs pushes on the cyclic stick, and the main rotors take us on
a magic carpet ride around the city, soaring above the Mississippi
River. Gibbs dips low over the water and pulls into a dramatic
climb. Our skids rise above the cantilevered bridge. I can see every
bolt in the structure as cars zoom through my high definition
frame. Next, Gibbs masterfully slides sideways so I can zoom into
the amazing house, with six strangers picked to live together and
have their lives filmed for MTV.

Gibbs moves me and the camera with the flare of a master
magician. The heart-pounding, G-pulling rocket ride has been
known to give directors sensory overload. More than one director
has become shell-shocked from the noise, the motion, and the

close proximity to death. Sometimes they can't speak. One director stared blankly when we asked him which shot to fly next. "I can't think," he mumbled. "You guys decide."

That's no problem. Gibbs and I have done this a thousand times. So I command Gibbs where to go next. "OK, Number Two. Let's go to the French Quarter and fly towards downtown."

"Negative Peanut Brain. I'll go where I want to go. You just point that camera where I tell you. I'm landing to refuel my aircraft."

God grant me strength. The bickering and insubordination never stops, except for a few moments when we pause to let the air traffic controllers talk.

Even as Gibbs lowers the collective to land, I work the Cineflex stick to squeeze the downtown skyline into frame with a thousand sparkling windshields on Interstate 10. When Alan Purwin flew for the hurricane, not a single car was moving there. But, now that the city has dried out, thousands of cars stream through my Cineflex frame.

As we refuel the helicopter, I stroll through Louis Armstrong Airport and hear a loud *BANG!!!* followed by a clown-like jingling sound. I follow the clown sounds to the first-class lounge, where millionaires relax between private jets. But instead of a first-class millionaire, I find Gibbs, red-faced. He looks like a trapped animal frozen in fear over a table that has no surface, just a million shards of shattered glass that have exploded and showered all over Gibbs' feet. In fact, glass chunks have scattered all over the room. Gibbs is holding a bouquet of flowers over the smashed table and seems afraid to move, in case another calamity might befall him.

I have no idea how he smashed the table to smithereens, in this place reserved for executives and heads-of-state. And where is the vase that the flowers came in?

"Gibbs! What did you do?! I can't take you anywhere..."

Gibbs looks like a dog who's been caught chewing fine furniture; he's absolutely guilty.

I gather my wind to read him the riot act for single-handedly ruining the first-class lounge, when he un-expectedly goes on the attack. "Don't give me that, Monkey Boy. You should be ashamed of what you did!"

"What I did?" I had nothing to do with this mess. Why doesn't he just apologize for ruining everything, like a bull in a china shop? Fortunately, God sent me to correct him in moments like this.

"I had nothing to do with this." I point to his feet, where a million pieces of glass form the tragic corpse of the executive coffee table.

But he persists. "You know what you did," he scolds. "You put the camera on the wrong side of the aircraft this morning and ruined our day."

OK. I did put the camera on the wrong side. But that's hardly relevant, since he blew apart the first-class lounge like an orangutan.

We haven't even cleaned up the glass from the table he smashed, and he's already changing the subject? I take a moment to patiently correct him.

"No one knows I did that thing with the camera. I'm going to have you arrested for vandalizing this coffee table."

But Gibbs continues, "Oh, they're gonna know what you did with the camera. Hand me my phone. I'm going to call the director and tell him what you did. Our poor director...I'm not going to let you ruin his day like that...he needs to know what you did, Peanut Brain. This is not good for you..."

In eighteen years, I've never gotten the last word in, even when Gibbs has done something spectacularly wrong. Somehow, he keeps an encyclopedic knowledge of my mess-ups and turns the discussion to something stupid I did before whatever stupid thing he did.

Then he turns to whomever we're working with, from film directors, to producers, pilots, waitresses, even the janitor of the first-class lounge, and he apologizes for *me*. He laments, as if he alone bears the never-ending burden of my existence — as if working with me is like trying to teach a monkey to do complicated math. Gibbs dramatically crowns me as if singing a country music song. "You're the King of the Dufuses, Dave."

God grant me strength. Everybody knows the computerized, gyro-stabilized cameras I operate are way more complicated than his aircraft, some of which were built before computers were invented.

Gibbs has a saying that makes no sense. "Dave, you could screw up a two-car funeral." I wish I had a nickel for every time he says that to me. But I don't know what it means. What in the Hell is a two-car funeral?

Gibbs never stops to explain why a funeral would only have two cars. He changes the subject and asks people if they've ever operated a gyro-stabilized camera. That's my job! He asks everyone we meet. If you've met Gibbs in any of the fifty states we've been to, you were likely offered my job.

Everyone he asks always says, "No." (Only a small number of people on Earth know how to operate a Cineflex.) But he's ready for their refusal, saying, "Don't worry." He points to me. "If Dave can do it, a monkey can do it. You'll figure out how to operate the Cineflex, and I won't even bring Dave next time."

In eighteen years of shooting with Gibbs, he's offered my job to everyone we've met, and then he apologizes for bringing me and promises not to bring me next time.

But Gibbs ALWAYS brings me next time. I've turned down more jobs with Gibbs than anyone else has offered me.

Together Gibbs and I fly The Super Bowl, The World Series, *Amazing Race*, *The Bachelor*, Monday Night Football, and everything in-between. We fly for every Network—ABC, CBS, NBC, MTV, Discovery, ESPN, HBO, FOX, Showtime, NatGeo, and even TMZ.

In eighteen years, Gibbs has opened countless doors. I can't do all the jobs he offers. But he always offers, and when I say, "No, thank you. I want to spend time with my family," he says, "OK Dave, well the job is yours if you want it."

God bless David Gibbs. He helps me to make the mortgage payment and spend time with my family. But he does have a funny thing about music.

MUSIC TO HIS EARS

G IBBS *ALWAYS* LISTENS TO MUSIC, everywhere we go. When we build a helicopter camera, he has a car nearby with the doors open to let the sound of easy-listening jazz echo through the cavernous aircraft hangar.

One thing I can't figure out is how he manages to find the same radio station in all fifty states. But somehow, he gets the exact same jazz orchestral music in every rental car in America.

Fortunately, God sent me to change the station. When I look over at Gibbs after I've found a new station, he looks like a man who's witnessed an unforgivable act of naked barbarism.

It's as if the Hindenburg crashed right in front of him with me at the controls. With righteous indignation, he reaches for the stereo with his bejeweled fingers to switch it back to easy listening. But sadly, he's baffled by the modern controls (invented after computers). So he turns every knob and pushes every button in a failed attempt to maneuver the rental car stereo back to easy-listening jazz.

One day after I changed the station from easy-listening to Brittany Spears, he whacks me on the arm as if I'm one of The Three Stooges, and then he struggles with the electronic menus of the stereo to try and get the radio back to easy-listening.

Apparently, Gibbs only knows how to use the car stereo in his old jeep. Stereos were simpler when they built that Jeep. New stereos like the one in this rental car have sophisticated features like electronic buttons that require you to be smarter than an eight-year-old.

Gibbs stares blankly at the fancy radio, which flashes

beautifully, but only fills the air with the sound of static mixed with Spanish-language programming. He can't figure it out. But he doesn't give up; he keeps turning dials and pushing buttons. Finally, his confusion turns to anger, and he makes a seething command. "Don't touch my radio again, you uncultured baboon!"

When he manages to get the rental car radio switched away from Britany Spears and back to easy-listening, he ceremoniously waves his hands as if conducting an orchestra. He acts as though he owns the car and has completely forgotten I'm even here.

And that's how we travel the world together. The arguments and dramatic feuding never stop, not even for a second.

BOTTOMLESS PIT

"**D**ON'T GIVE ME THAT CRAP. That's a bunch of crap!" Gibbs says while flying through the skyscrapers of San Francisco. He says he doesn't like my idea to put the Transamerica building like a rifle-sight in front of Pac Bell Park. He points to himself as if he's painting the Sistine Chapel, and I'm just here to clean his paint splatters off the floor.

"You point that camera where I tell you." He then gestures to the Transamerica Building, which he's perfectly aligned with Pac Bell Park like a rifle-sight. Behind the iconic building is where the Giants are playing in the World Series. Gibbs and I argue about everything, even when we agree completely. Now he hovers a thousand feet in the air, exactly as I told him. But he commands me to keep quiet while he paints his canvas.

I pull back on the Cineflex joystick and find the skyscraper spire wrapped in the clouds that are swirling just above the edge of the ballpark.

"Look at chopper!" the director screams at his crew to put our shot online as fourteen million people come back from World Series commercials.

"Three, two, one—dissolve chopper!" the director counts us onto the air in front of the biggest audience in baseball.

Gibbs pushes forward on the cyclic stick and we float over the top of the building, revealing the clouds and the stadium. It's poetry in motion.

Back at home no one knows I'm flying over the World Series. My neighbors don't even know who Gibbs is. I never talk about my work. When Gibbs and I pack up the Cineflex after the ball game, all I want to do is to get back to the peace and quiet of Sky Forest.

When I arrive on Cloud Nine, I walk through the trees to the Post Office. In a tiny room, I find our PO Box and check the mail, but there's something wrong in my mail box. There are bills for something I never bought. So I call the company. "I don't have an account. Why are you sending me bills?" I can't figure out why bills started showing up for trash service we didn't ask for and have never used. How is this even possible?

The woman on the phone at the trash company laughs. I believe I can hear her smiling as she says, "If you live here, we're billing you. And if you don't pay it, the county will take your house."

Why is she laughing? That's messed up.

I look online and discover that San Bernardino County politicians have set the garbage service up so that every homeowner gets a trash bill, even if no one lives in the house. Even if you haul your own trash like I do, you have to pay for their trash service (and word on the street is, the county politicians get some of the money.)

Even if no one lives in the house, you'll get a trash bill, and if you don't pay it, the politicians will steal your house. So my neighbors dutifully put their trash on the street for the crooked trash service. But the trash isn't there when the trash guys show up, because the bears have opened the cans and eaten half of the trash. Their big bear bellies are full of household items and the rest of the trash is strewn through the neighborhood.

This unhealthy clown circus repeats every two weeks, because corrupt politicians must have their money. And to Hell with the people and animals that are harmed in the process.

One of the reasons I bought a home in the forest was to get away from big-city dangers like corruption. I'm surprised we can still be ripped off by people down in the crime-ridden city below, but I know why they get away with it. Everyone knows you can't fight city hall...

DEADLIEST CATCH

T WO THOUSAND MILES AWAY FROM Sky Forest, a helicopter pilot points to an Alaskan crab-fishing boat buried in the black sand of a volcanic beach.

Discovery Channel
DEADLIEST CATCH

I have never seen anything like the surreal landscape below our helicopter. If Dr. Seuss had a bad acid trip, he might draw a picture like the one in my Wescam viewfinder. The human ship is sunken to its wheelhouse in black earth. This is the boat to nowhere, run aground, six hundred miles from the nearest human city.

We land and walk around the ghost ship. If this is man vs. nature, then nature won.

I'm as far away from Los Angeles as I can get. The only skyscraper is a smoking volcano.

We are here to work on a new Discovery Channel show about Alaskan crab fishermen. The entombed boat tells me that if anything bad happens, we may be lost and forgotten.

TV's Mike Rowe stands on the shipwreck to start the show and introduce the audience to a place where, if you run aground, you might never be found...

Rowe climbs into the crow's nest of the sand-sunken boat and talks to my camera as my pilot circles the earth-locked shipwreck with his Bell 206b helicopter. Mike Rowe welcomes the audience to the first season of *Deadliest Catch* with a "stand-up" talk where he explains what's happening out on Bering Sea crab boats, like The Northwestern, helmed by Captain Sig Hansen.

My pilot pulls left on his cyclic stick, and we pull away from Mike. The cold Bering Sea waves crash on the beach that stretches for a hundred miles without humans, except Mike Rowe. The ocean and the earth claimed the boat under Mike's feet. It's a perfect way to introduce the audience to the world of *Deadliest Catch*.

Next, we fly to an abandoned Alaskan town where everyone was killed by a tsunami. The town is high upon a cliff, but somehow the tidal wave climbed the cliff and killed everyone. The sole survivor, they say, is a man who happened to be checking a generator high above the town when the ocean swallowed every living soul.

That was the end of the town. Now the ruined buildings sit empty, just like the boat to nowhere. I've seen ghost towns before, places where boom and bust caused everyone to move away, but this is an actual ghost town where all of the residents died at the same time.

The eerie town offers shelter from the ruthless Alaskan wind so we can service the helicopter. To get to the Alaskan crab fisherman, we're crossing over a thousand miles of empty Dr. Seuss wasteland. There are no human cities and no airports, just black sand, ghosts, and shipwrecks.

When we finally make it to the old WWII Army airstrip in Dutch Harbor, we land and shut down the engine, but we can't get out because the howling Bering Sea winds are pushing the blades so fast they won't stop spinning. Even though we stopped the engine five minutes ago, the blades are wind-milling at almost flight-gate. I say, "Do you want me to get out and stop the blades?"

He thinks carefully and says, "Yeah. Go ahead."

I jump out and grab the tail rotor shaft to stop the main rotor blades. It takes a while because the screaming winds are driving the main rotors with the force of a hurricane. But finally, I wrestle the helicopter blades to a standstill.

My pilot steps out of the aircraft, looks up at the blades, and back at me, with my hand still gripping the tail rotor.

"Who taught you to do that?" he asks.

"No one," I say. "I just did it."

His eyes grow wide. "Well, let me show you how to do it so you don't lose your arm next time!"

He waddles back to where I'm standing. My pilot is a classic Alaskan bush man, rugged and salty. He grabs the tail rotor to show me how not to do it because this method is certain death, but he's showing exactly how I did it. Thank God for guardian angels.

We tie down the blades to keep the vicious winds from spinning them again. We jack the little Jet Ranger up on wheels and push it into a rotting World War II hangar.

It's cold, wet, and dark. There's no electricity or heat. The only sound is the massive WWII bomber doors slamming in the howling winds. *Whack! Wham! Rattle...* What in the world are we doing in this weather-beaten middle-of-nowhere?

I look at my cell phone — no signal. I've lost all connection to the civilized world. We're on a frozen island in the middle of the vast Bering Sea.

I don't know what we're going to see here, but whatever it is, no one has ever seen it before. Of all the billions of humans on Planet Earth, a tiny few have made it to this half-frozen wasteland.

On the way in, we passed a capsized tanker ship. Under the sea water with the sunken ship is a Coast Guard helicopter that crashed while attempting to rescue the ship's crew. There's a lot of danger here, and not a lot of help in case of emergency... sometimes, even the rescuers don't make it out alive.

Our presence in the old hangar draws a crowd of Coast Guard guys, who gather around our tiny helicopter with looks of shock and awe. "You guys are going out there in *that?*" one of them asks in disbelief.

"Yes," I say matter-of-factly. The looks on their faces tell me they expect to never see us again. One of them offers, "It's so sketchy here, our pilots have to check in by radio every ten minutes, so we know they're still alive..."

Welcome to Dutch Harbor, Alaska.

The Coast Guard guys speak of the power of nature with awe and respect. They should. This place is deadly. But their helicopter is three times our size. They have two engines, with many times the power of our little Allison turbine, and their helicopter crashed and sank to the bottom of the Bering Sea.

If our engine fails over the frozen Bering Sea, we'll die almost instantly. In this remote wilderness we'll probably never be found, just like that boat to nowhere in the sand; we'll be forgotten in a lost world.

The sunken Coast Guard Jayhawk helicopter has heated blades and instruments so they can fly through the frozen storms. Our helicopter has nothing. No wonder the Coast Guard guys are afraid for us.

There are no trees in Dutch Harbor, just freezing seawater, mud, and winds that sometimes go over a hundred miles an hour. If Hell froze over and had a fishing dock, it would look like this.

Looks of shock and awe are common here. On opening day of crab season, I witness a gathering of TV producers listening to radio traffic with frantic messages of boats and fisherman lost at sea. I see expressions change as cool, calm documentary producers realize that the boat, with our people on it, might be the one that sank last night.

It turns out a partner of the show's boats capsized and sank so quickly they never got a distress call out. Poor souls. Six men lost their lives on Season One of *Deadliest Catch*.

DON'T COME HOME

ACK IN SUNNY LOS ANGELES, I kiss my fiancé and go to work with Gibbs.

"I love you."

"I love you too."

"See you later."

My fiancé is the smartest and funniest woman I've ever met. I know I can count on her when the going gets tough. And I know she'll never do anything to hurt Wyatt. We have a wonderful life.

With a spring in my step, I bound to the airport, where Gibbs is waiting to give me a ration of shit (and help me build the Cineflex Camera). Without asking, Gibbs grabs my wrenches and starts assembling camera parts. When the camera's built, he dons a flight helmet and lights the Lycoming gas turbine with the skill of 35 years of flying airplanes and helicopters. He meticulously advances the throttle to bring the turbine up to an ear-splitting fifty thousand rpm. He pulls the collective lever, pushes the cyclic stick forward, and we rise into the sky. Gibbs points for the director of *The Amazing Race* to see the homes of Hollywood celebrities as they pass beneath our skids and into our tape recorder.

Gibbs knows every street and neighborhood in Los Angeles. "We chased OJ down this street. We shot a movie on that street." The director *ooh*'s and *aah*'s as Gibbs takes us on a guided tour of Tinsel Town. Meanwhile, I'm framing landmarks with the gyro-stabilized Cineflex. The director falls silent as he watches fifty miles of concrete and palm trees swirl poetically in the Cineflex frame. It's overwhelming. The most typical reaction we get from TV directors is stunned silence and sensory overload.

But Gibbs is not satisfied. "Peanut Head! Put my camera on those surfers."

What's wrong with him? A driver can't tell a cameraman what to do. So I correct him.

"It's Mr. Peanut Head to you." Having re-established my authority, I push the Cineflex stick to form a steady frame around the surfers, who are riding waves in the California sun. Gibbs lowers the collective and we descend to palm tree-height above Santa Monica Beach.

"Tower, we're going feet-wet!" Gibbs waxes poetic with air traffic control as he lowers the collective again to bring us inches above the breaking waves.

Gibbs accelerates to a hundred and thirty miles per hour and catapults us into the sky. Ocean waves drop like an animated curtain to reveal the City of Los Angeles.

Gibbs leaves the Pacific Ocean behind and rockets around the sparkling downtown buildings. I zoom in on people sitting at their cubicle desks inside marble and glass towers.

As the California sun turns golden, and office workers climb in their cars, they sit in gridlock traffic. But Gibbs zooms a hundred miles an hour above their bumper-to-bumper jam.

For just a moment, I take my eyes off the Cineflex and look out the window. A hundred stories below my feet, fifteen million people slog away at their jobs and sit in traffic. Their brake lights form a jam of humanity that glistens in the ethereal stillness of the Cineflex viewfinder.

I'm lucky to sit up here with Gibbs.

We use every drop of sunlight as we fly and film into the night. Another dream-like day ends as I climb into my pickup truck. Gibbs and I quit arguing for a moment as I shake his hand and thank him for a safe ride.

Now I'm excited because I get to go home to the fiancé and baby Wyatt. Wyatt's mom is a classic beauty with a wicked sense of humor, and Wyatt is one of the cutest and most social babies I've ever seen. We have a great little family, in a home filled with love.

But something is off tonight. The fiancé sounds weird and says something I'll never forget. "Don't come home."

"What do you mean don't come home?" I ask.

"I can't be in a relationship with you anymore."

"What!?"

It's surreal, and it takes my breath away. This bizarre shocking news comes like a bolt of lightning.

We get along great. We rarely fought in our two years together. We have a baby and are engaged to be married. But suddenly, she sounds as if we'd never met. It's as though she's taking out the trash and it's just a chore she wants to be done with. She says matter-of-factly that I shouldn't come home ever again.

So of course I come home.

What follows is a very odd conversation. She's indignant. "What are you doing here? I told you, I don't love you anymore. Get out."

I feel like one of those poor whales swimming happily in the ocean, when a man with a harpoon cannon shoots it from behind. One minute I'm swimming along, and the next minute a cold steel spear, from somewhere I can't see, drives right through my heart. I'm struck by a force I did not see coming.

I point to our bedroom. "Our little one is sleeping in there. We can fix anything you don't like."

But she's not listening. She just drones, "I don't love you. Get out."

Whatever this is, I must be partly to blame. I've made a lot of mistakes in my life, but this one is spectacular.

I think about this whirlwind of evil ripping our family apart, and say, "No. I want more kids."

She explodes. "What?!!! I just told you I don't love you!"

"So what? People who don't love each other have sex all the time." (I realize this might not have been the most logical next step.)

But I haven't changed. My life and my entire world revolves around her. I don't have anywhere else I want to be. We have a family together. She said we could have more kids. These are lifelong plans.

Wyatt's mom and I are supposed to get married and make Wyatt a little brother or a sister. What's going on now?

She may have moved on, but I haven't. I still have all the same dreams and feelings for her as I did this morning when I went to work. I love her unconditionally, and all my future plans include her, even if she's in a strange mood (which has happened before, now that I think about it).

But she leaves with Wyatt and doesn't tell me where she's taking him. It's the first time in Wyatt's life that he can't be with his mom and dad. He's an innocent baby, and this is dark. This is evil.

FAMILY TIES

Our house is empty and I'm alone. For the second time in my life, I'm completely heart-broken. It's like when my mom died, except death didn't take Wyatt's mom. She chose to leave.

I need to know what's going on. When she ran off she left her laptop on the kitchen counter. So, for the first time since we met, I open her laptop and peer inside. Her web browser is open with email logged in. What I find in her computer is unbelievable. I see emails going back several months with her parents. Unbeknownst to me, they've been plotting to get rid of me and break up our family.

Then I see an email to a lawyer. She says she's "planning to leave my fiancé and it's not going to go well." She knows how much I love her. She knows I cherish our life together. Maybe that's why she said, "it's not going to go well."

The train wreck takes my breath away. One minute everything's fine.

"I love you."

"I love you too."

The next minute my family is gone, and I don't know where they went.

After a few days she agrees to come home and let me see Wyatt. Wyatt's a happy baby. He doesn't cry or scream, he just smiles and giggles. It helps me forget that his mom wants our family to be ripped apart.

My behavior next probably makes no sense to thinking people. Wyatt's mom won't let us live together anymore, so I'm sleeping in my truck down the street. That way I can see Wyatt when he wakes up in the morning.

My new routine is surreal. I wake up in the bed of my pickup truck, walk over, and knock on the door at the house where I used to live. I put Wyatt in his carrier and take him out of the house so mom can sleep in. Wyatt and I walk to the grocery store and buy his mom flowers and her favorite foods. I know it's weird, but Wyatt and I have done this every day since he was born.

A friend hears about this. He's flabbergasted. "Maybe you should stop bringing her flowers..."

My friends give good advice. So I quit bringing her flowers and food. It seems strange not to buy her things that make her happy. But I always take advice.

THEY DON'T LOVE HER
LIKE YOU DO...

WYATT'S GRANDMA AND GRANDPA LIVE in FL and rarely come to see us, so I made a picture frame to help them feel connected to their grandson. Wyatt's grandma sent me a nice thank you note for the pictures. She didn't say a word that anything was wrong. Grandma and grandpa never raised a single concern, like "Hey Dave, our daughter said there's a problem and we want you guys to work it out."

They could've brought me anything. There was nothing I wouldn't give up or change to make her happy and keep our family together. But I was never given a warning or a chance. Now I'm reading an email from grandma where they're secretly plotting to tear our family apart and get rid of me. Grandma says, "Don't worry. If Dave takes the car back, dad says we'll get you a new one."

When I met Wyatt's mom, I let her drive one of my cars so she could get out of debt. Knowing they're about to unleash Hell on me, they're worried, but not about me and Wyatt. They're worried I'll take my car back when I discover their cold-hearted betrayal.

My friends come to check on me. One of them hears about grandma's car email. He thinks for a quick second and says something that shocks me. "Take the car."

"What?" I love Wyatt's mom unconditionally, and the thought of her needing something like food or transportation is unthinkable. But my friend says, "Take the car and watch what happens."

"What do you mean?"

"Her parents don't love her like you do. They're not going to buy her a car."

I don't get it, but I'm lucky I have smart friends who see things I can't.

When she comes home to get some things, she turns to get back in my car and leave again with Wyatt. I climb in the back seat with Wyatt like I used to do when we're together.

She screams, "What are you doing? Get out!"

"No." I say. "You can break up our family, but I won't support this. You're not doing it in my car." She panics, yelling, screaming, and shoving. After her violent melt-down, she puts baby Wyatt in a taxi and leaves my car behind.

Now grandma and grandpa can buy her a car like they promised. They can all live happily ever after without me...right?

Wrong. She comes crawling back the next day. She says her mom and dad had offered to buy her a car, but when she asked for the money, they said they're having "financial problems." They won't buy her a car as promised.

My friend was right about her parents. I'm glad I took his advice. Grandma and grandpa are helping to get rid of a good man and provider. And in less than a week, they're already back-pedaling on their promise to provide for her in my place. Now she has no car.

So I do what I've always done. I take care of her. I sell my car to her for half its blue-book value. It's not the hard-ball my friend told me to play, but it makes me happy to see Wyatt and his mom in a nice, big, safe car again. Anyway, my friend was right about the grandparents.

I talk to Gibbs about what's happening with my family. My life suddenly sounds like a country music song. Gibbs listens thoughtfully. He's supportive, but he doesn't cling to hope like me. Somehow he knows that she won't allow our family back together.

Maybe Gibbs is right about me. I *could* screw up a two-car funeral.

My happy family life with the fiancé and Wyatt is taken away. She sues so I can't see Wyatt. It breaks my heart when Wyatt can't be with his mom and his dad.

Nuts.

SLEEPING LIKE A BABY

B ABIES DON'T KNOW HOW TO sleep. They don't know what sleep is. When Wyatt gets tired, he panics because his eyes fail, and his body suddenly stops working with him in it.

At night mom lets Wyatt cry himself to sleep, but I always hold him until he falls asleep, which turns his nightly panic attacks into peace and comfort.

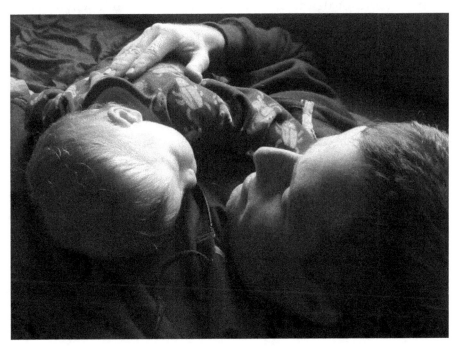

As Wyatt's tiny body collapses, he panics. You or I would just go to sleep, but he's a baby and doesn't know what sleep is. He rubs his little eyes, which suddenly won't stay open. So I hug him, put him on my chest. He immediately calms down. His whole body relaxes. He yawns, lays his head down, and is asleep in seconds. That's all it takes. Once he feels safe and protected, he can let his body relax.

One evening at mom's house, Wyatt is screaming in his crib. This is normally when I would comfort him to sleep, but not tonight. Wyatt's Grandma has come out from Florida. Grandma has replaced me, and I have to leave.

As I walk down the stairs leading to the streets of Los Angeles, I can hear Wyatt screaming all the way to my truck as Mom and grandma leave him alone to cry himself to sleep. His screaming fills the air in the neighborhood as the last light leaves the sky, and the city falls to darkness.

It breaks my heart when Wyatt isn't allowed to see me because it's "not your night."

In a world of deadbeat dads, I can't understand why anyone would throw a dad out of the house.

EXHIBIT A

WYATT'S MOM IS TAKING ME to court, but I decide not to hire a lawyer. I'm defending myself.

I know it's not a good idea, but my life is full of bad ideas that feel right.

I don't have a lawyer, but I want to show the judge how much I love spending time with my little one. So I make a picture book for the judge, entitled "Life is Good," Exhibit A. It's a beautiful coffee table book....and the beginning of a most unconventional child-custody case.

I was right about Wyatt. He's a beautiful gift, and he loves his life. I might not get my way in court, but I'll send a positive message. I love spending time with my son. In all of Wyatt's life, I've never missed a day with him. I never make plans that don't include him.

Wyatt's mom never asks if I want him on her days, just, "Are you in town?" Because if I'm in town, I always take him, whether it's my day or not. I've gladly taken him every single night mom doesn't want him. I love every second of my time with Wyatt.

Remember when Wyatt was an unexpected gift? I was the one who wanted him. That's not just my opinion, it's the only way I can explain what's happening now. While mom is fighting me in court to keep me away from Wyatt (which is a way to get money for child support), she constantly leaves Wyatt at my house on her days.

On Mother's Day, I receive a text that I'll never forget. It's from Wyatt's mother. She says she's tired and asks if I will just keep him today instead of bringing him to her house like we planned. I wish I could say I'm shocked, but I'm not. This happens all the time. I'm sad for her and Wyatt, but have no problem adjusting my schedule to keep Wyatt on Mother's Day.

I explain to the people I'm with that the plan has changed, and little Wyatt will be with us today. I watch their expressions change, and their eyes fill with sadness at the idea that Wyatt's Mother doesn't even want to see him on Mother's Day, but Wyatt charges into the room and causes a mini-riot. Even among jaded grownups, he gets a laugh with his fun, fearless energy.

But the next day we hit a wall. Wyatt's preschool calls me. It's not my day to have Wyatt, but somehow they knew to call me. "Hi David. We just want you to know that Wyatt is in tears. We're having a Mother's Day party, and all the moms are here except Wyatt's mom. She didn't come."

Everyone feels bad for Wyatt. I do too. No problem. I drop what I'm doing and drive to Wyatt's preschool. I pick him up and we spend an awesome day together. You might wonder, if Wyatt's mom doesn't want to spend time with him, why she's suing me to keep me away from him? I'll let you do the math on that. I'm just happy to have Wyatt with me today.

LAWYERS

I'M NOT BRINGING A LAWYER. I'm bringing a picture book, made with love. This may not go well.

Lawyers know how to do court stuff, and I don't, so I drive to downtown LA to watch some trials and learn to put my best foot forward with the judge.

The courthouse is intimidating. Just getting in requires commitment. I have to wait in line with people you wouldn't want to meet in a dark alley. Thugs have been arrested for violent crimes and are coming for their day in court. They tried to dress up, but their heinous tattoos poke through cheap suits and freshly combed hair. You can try to put lipstick on a pig; it looks like a lot of pigs are getting their day in court. Here they come, disguised as decent people.

Their nice clothes and slicked back hair look like backward Halloween costumes. Instead of nice people dressed as monsters, I see monsters dressed up as nice people. This is a hurried effort to fool the judge after they've lied, stolen, stabbed, robbed, abused women, children, and small animals. Seeing them all cleaned up for the judge makes me wonder how different they looked when they were drunk, on drugs, fighting, hitting their girlfriends and all the other things that land you in a maximum-security courthouse.

After the X-rays, metal detectors, and well-dressed thugs, I wander through the endless halls of LA Superior Court, where lawyers speak a different language and dictate to the little people.

I find a family courtroom, sneak in, and sit down. I take a nervous breath, afraid to make a sound or distract anyone from court proceedings. In front of the judge, a husband and wife argue back and forth, taking turns on the witness stand. Clearly they hate each other and have been before the judge many times.

He says, "Your honor! I want to stipulate that she is crazy!" and labors back to his seat as if exhausted by his ex-wife and mother of his children. She steams to the witness stand like a heat-seeking missile. "Your honor! I have migraines because of him and have to take antidepressants because of what he did at the kids' school!"

They're furious and relentless. They seem to have spent all their money on lawyers and are now left on their own to argue back and forth in front of the judge without lawyers. It looks like neither of them have had a good night's sleep since they broke up years ago.

The judge braces his head in his hands as their furious words hammer his temples. Now he has to figure out what to do with them and the kids. He looks like a man watching in disgust as a pack of lions eat their own cubs.

The judge takes a deep breath and grips his forehead as if in pain. The ex-wife caterwauls about dad and schools and money, interrupted by her ex-husband arguing back at her.

The judge seems exhausted by them and announces a recess. Everyone in the courtroom gets up to leave.

I stand and turn to the door when suddenly, the judge calls a stop to the entire court room. Out of a crowd of fifty people he points to me and says, "Why are you here?"

Everyone freezes in mid-exit. The bustling courtroom comes to a complete halt. To my horror, everyone in the courtroom stops what they're doing and turns to stare at me. I freeze, afraid to say a word. His Honor breaks the awkward silence and speaks for me, "Are you here to watch?"

"Yes." I say nervously. "I have a family law case, and I'm representing myself."

"OK. I just want you to know you can stay here as long as you want. You can come back after recess and watch some more."

That's crazy! The judge stopped the entire courtroom to pick me out of the crowd and make me feel welcome.

FEEDING FRENZY

DURING THE RECESS, I WANDER up to the cafeteria on the top floor of the lavish LA Superior Court Building, where lawyers sit overlooking the little people of Los Angeles.

I've flown over this building a thousand times. It's one of the ivory towers under our skids. But now I get to see what's inside.

What's inside is very strange. There are more cases being decided in the cafeteria than in court.

Opposing lawyers talk over tuna melts.

"How are the kids?"

"How's your golf game?"

"How do you like the new BMW 3 Series?"

"So, what are you thinking on Smith vs. Smith?"

These courtroom adversaries are fighting a hotly-contested feud between bitter clients, but they talk like old friends. In fact, they don't act like adversaries at all. They seem to be on the same side—the side with the money.

"Look Bob, Mr. Smith spent $100,000 on his girlfriend's apartment, and he has a vacation he wants to take with the kids. You know what the judge is going to say. Let's just do $4,000 per month alimony and $1,800 child support."

"OK. That's reasonable. I'll tell him. Tell your client we'll do those numbers, but she has to move out of the Malibu property, because Mr. Smith won't bend on that."

And just like that, the legal war is over without firing a shot in the most casual, matter-of-fact way. Having worked out the hostile litigation, opposing lawyers go back to biting their sandwiches, paid for by Mr. and Mrs. Smith. The topic turns to more passionate subjects like their tuna melts and what kind of boat they're buying for the lake house, which is near the other lawyer's lake house.

They say justice is blind, but lawyers aren't. They see money. Lawyers see those who want something and are willing to pay. It's not really my lawyer against your lawyer. It's both lawyers for sale.

Three lawyers (counting the judge) are in charge of everything. All three lawyers win, no matter what happens in the case. And when the clients are gone, and new clients come in, it'll be the same three lawyers billing both sides and having lunch at their expense. It's not a *bad* system of deciding things, but I was expecting something nobler in a building with a three-story statue of a goddess holding the scales of justice, as if nothing matters but the weight of evidence. The truth is, the scales are full of money.

I know I'm approaching my child custody case in an idealistic way. Simple-mindedness gets me into trouble every single time. I believed in the court's statue of that goddess holding the scales of justice, letting the weight of evidence decide each case, but what I find in that courthouse are flawed human beings who've set themselves up to profit from every step, regardless of the outcome.

I return to the courtroom after lunch and learn that lawyers always get their say, no matter what. A feisty lawyer has already finished arguing, and the judge moved on to other matters. But that doesn't stop her from interrupting. "Your Honor! May I be heard on this matter!? May I be heard on this matter!? May I be heard on this matter!?" She just keeps saying it like a broken record until the judge finally stops what he's doing and allows her to speak.

The relentless lawyer opens up a new can of worms for the case. The judge sets everything aside and just wants to know if anyone feels strongly and wants to argue. That's good, I suppose, if you want to add billable hours.

One thing that seems unlimited is billable hours. Have you ever noticed that lawyers drive expensive cars? I notice that the clients always end up without lawyers after a certain number of court hearings. Very few people can spend hundreds of thousands of dollars to win a fight with their bitter ex who has their lawyer arguing about everything under the sun. Eventually, one or both parents run out of money, and they stand alone before the judge, just like the fire-breathing couple I saw earlier.

Don't these parents know they're still together? They're bonded by their children, and their children need care and feeding until they're eighteen. This legal circus means nothing in the grand scheme of things. The kids will need help all their lives and their mom and dad will always be their mom and dad. Lawyers can't undo that.

I DON'T MAKE AS MUCH MONEY AS PEOPLE THINK

RRRRR-*Poof!* Back in Sky Forest, my tired old truck dry-heaves and spits smoke. Wyatt watches a familiar cloud of grey smoke engulf the truck. He hugs my arm from his child safety seat as we enter the daily adventure of "Will the truck start?"

Oh man. I really hope the truck starts. We have a long way to go today. But the truck isn't starting, and the battery's running low. I may run out of starting electricity and options. This'll leave Wyatt and I stranded at Cloud Nine.

After twenty minutes, the weary battery finally turns the old engine one last time, and a massive cloud of smoke billows from the tailpipe as one cylinder chokes to life, dragging the other seven cylinders with it in a reluctant precession. The quiet of Sky Forest gives way to choking and smoking as our engine awakens. "Hooray!" We celebrate the miracle that allows us to drive down the mountain to Los Angeles.

Wyatt hugs my arm all the way there until I drop him off at the preschool his mom enrolled him in.

At the airport, Gibbs talks about helicopter accidents like the one that killed his mentor, a movie pilot named Rick Holley. Rick was killed when he crashed into power lines while flying a camera for a movie. One minute they were sky kings, and the next they were falling to their deaths. The laws of physics take no prisoners at our office in the sky.

We have a dangerous job. It pays well, but I only work a day

115

per show, and the rest of the time, I'm unemployed. I make good money, but only for a day here and there. It's hard to earn a living this way. Over the years, I've taught many people how to do my job, but so far, none of them have been able to make enough money to live on.

I'm often attacked and taken advantage of because people think my job has made me wealthy. The truth is, I'm a single dad trying to make ends meet. I drive an old truck with 280,000 miles on it. The truck has bald tires. I thank God every time I turn the key, and it starts. It's all I can do to keep things running.

In the city, Wyatt and I live with our friends. It's the only way we can make ends meet.

I love my life, but it's a simple life.

CLOUD EIGHT

"P AN RIGHT, YOU'RE SHOOTING THE wrong house." Our director commands from the front seat of our helicopter next to Gibbs. We're looking down on a billion-dollar cliff-side neighborhood in Malibu. When I see the home, I'm blown away. This house is bigger and more impressive than all the other multi-million-dollar estates we filmed for *The Real Housewives of Beverly Hills*.

"Pan right Dave. That's the guest house." I'm stunned to discover that the biggest and most beautiful home I've ever seen is merely the *guest quarters* for an even bigger house. When I finally get to the main house, the building needs its own zip code. The family property is an entire mountainside in Malibu. The Pacific Ocean looks like their private swimming pool. Gibbs goes right to work circling the sprawling estate with the helicopter, so I can zoom in and out of the impressive front door.

As the sun sets over the ocean, we keep filming. We shoot Malibu, Beverly Hills, Hollywood, and everything in between. Gibbs and I never waste a second in the air. Even when he is landing at 9:00 pm, I'm still searching the city lights with our powerful zoom lens to paint what Gibbs calls "My Canvas."

As the director puts a stack of shot tapes into his car and drives away, I turn to Gibbs. "You're released, Number Two. Take the rest of the day off." (It's now 10:00 pm)

In all the years I've known Gibbs, I don't think he ever let me say a word without correcting me.

"Negative, Monkey Boy. I'm not going to leave you

unsupervised." He waves his arms dramatically, as if he's a school-master chiding an errant school-boy.

And with that, Gibbs steals a few of my wrenches and spends the next two hours unbolting the Cineflex Camera. Piece by piece, he patiently helps me pack the high-tech movie machine into boxes.

The camera weighs several hundred pounds. I still have to pack it up and drive it to the camera house and drop it off. It's a herculean task, but I never ask Gibbs to help me because it's not his job, and after an exhausting day of flying, I don't want him to deal with late-night heavy-lifting.

"You're released Number Two." I announce again. I point to the hangar exit so he can go home and go to sleep.

"Negative Peanut Head," he says. "I'm not going to leave you unsupervised." He always speaks to me as if correcting a toddler.

As I drive to the camera house, Gibbs' headlights hit the back of my head. He follows me in his old Jeep to help lift the heavy camera cases into the camera house, insulting me at every step. I lock up the darkened building and Gibbs, and I stand in the empty parking lot. It's midnight, and we finally have the only serious discussion we ever have. I grab his hand and give it a shake. I look squarely into his mischievous eyes and say, "Thanks for the safe ride." Gibbs and I have had this conversation over a thousand times. I tell him thank you after every day we enter the sky, and he brings me safely back to Earth.

When I finally drive up the dirt road to our home in the city, it's long past Wyatt's bedtime, but Wyatt is already snug in his bed. My friends at Cloud Eight fed him dinner while I was working. They bathed him, put him into pajamas, and tucked him into bed long before my headlight beams turned up the dirt road to our trailer.

When Wyatt's mom threw me out of our house, my friends rescued us.They offered to let Wyatt and I park our little RV in their driveway so we'd have a place to live in the city.

If I hadn't bought the RV for Switch the Dog, I don't know where we'd sleep. But here we are, safe and snuggled in Switch's trailer at my friend's house. Baby Wyatt and I moved into our RV when his mom "fell out of love" with me. We've lived in Switch's trailer, for seven years now.

I call it Cloud Eight. It's my happy place, one notch below Cloud Nine. Inside our trailer is smaller than the kitchen at Cloud Nine. The little RV fits inside a car parking lot space.

The help we receive from our friends at Cloud Eight has made all the difference. While Gibbs and I are out flying, our friends pick Wyatt up from school, feed him, and make sure he gets to bed on time. They treat him like a member of their family. Life is good. We are loved. We are blessed.

The owner of Cloud Eight is the oldest of seven brothers, and he's a consummate big brother, surveying the tiny parking space-sized home that Wyatt and I share in his driveway. He checks on our living space and our spirits, asking about me and Wyatt. "How are you? How's the little man? How's work?" And then he says something that floors me.

He says that the small amount of money I pay to rent the space in his driveway helps his family keep their house. They have one of those crazy adjustable-rate mortgages that keeps going up. The increasing mortgage payments have pushed them to the brink of foreclosure.

But the small amount of money we pay for rent saved them from the financial calamity that drove many people into foreclosure during the Great Recession. I'm amazed that the kindness they have shown us would have an unexpected benefit that could mean so much to their family.

The trailer we live in is smaller than most people's closets, but for me and Wyatt, it's the perfect home, where we share everything with our friends. Wyatt's mom lives alone, and often calls me to help her find child care. Even when I'm out of town, she sends Wyatt to Cloud Eight, where our friends care for him.

I tried to buy a home in the city for me and Wyatt, but the only house I can afford is in a gang-infested neighborhood. I can't find anything I can afford where I'd feel safe raising Wyatt. By contrast, our home at Cloud Eight is safe, quiet, and filled with friends who treat us like family.

I think that's a great lesson for Wyatt. When he grows up and bad things happen in his life, he can go it alone in a cruel world, or he can share with his friends and family. I end my search for a home in the asphalt jungle, and I begin looking for a bigger RV, so Wyatt can have room to grow at Cloud Eight.

GUARDIAN ANGEL

I SEE AN AD IN THE RV Trader that looks too good to be true. It's for a great big RV at a low price. I call, and a man named Duane calls back to ask which ad I'm looking at, because he just dropped the price $10,000 and wants to make sure I have the new, lower price — amazing.

Most people would negotiate for the highest price possible, but Duane and his family want to make sure we get a cheaper price for their RV.

When I meet Duane, I discover that his RV is five times the size of Switch's RV and exactly what our family needs — room to grow.

It's the nicest RV trailer I've ever seen, with separate rooms for me and Wyatt. I offer to buy it on the spot, but it's too big for my pickup truck to pull to Cloud Eight. The massive rig weighs 20,000 pounds, and I need a heavy-duty diesel truck to pull it.

Duane knows I have no way to take it home. He thinks for a moment and calls his wife to ask her how to handle the predicament. I can tell that Duane has a very caring family. He says his wife has a plan. They'll give me time to buy a bigger truck, and Duane's wife told him to give us his fifth-wheel trailer hitch from his truck. The hitch is a very expensive item, and this unexpected gift is a huge help to our little family.

I know we only need to move the RV once or twice, so I search Craigslist for an old beat-up diesel pickup truck and find a Ford with 203,000 miles on it. It's beat to hell and missing some parts. The roof leaks and the ceiling dangles loosely above our heads — perfect!

I don't waste time with a mechanic's inspection, I just hand the owner a wad of cash and drive home in the biggest and loudest pickup truck I've ever seen.

You're supposed to put toddlers in the back seat, but I can't put Wyatt in the backseat because there is no backseat. Wyatt has to sit beside me in the front, and he loves it! I love it too. Riding in the old beater truck with Wyatt instantly becomes my favorite thing to do.

That's how an old beater pickup truck became our favorite thing on four wheels. Driving the old truck isn't just a gap in time between activities. It's an activity I share with my son. I only intended to drive the big diesel truck one time, but it's become our primary transportation, because we love sitting side-by-side. Wyatt hugs my arm all the way to Orange County to get Duane's giant RV.

Duane and his family patiently wait while I buy the truck and install Duane's hitch in it. When we drive to get the Big RV, Duane's wife and daughter are there to help us. They're extremely careful with everything. Duane shows me how to care for the generator, and he pumps up the tires for us.

Duane's wife, Angela, takes a protective role over Wyatt the minute she lays eyes on him. She makes it clear she won't allow some yahoo to drive little Wyatt in an unsafe manner, so she makes me practice backing up the huge trailer to prove I can drive it to Cloud Eight without crashing. Of all the RV ads, I found the one family that spends hours helping us hook up the RV and puts us through their own driving safety class.

Pulling the massive RV is unlike anything I've ever done. It's like dragging a building down the street. It has the same turn radius as HMS Titanic. I discover that driving the massive rig into a gas station is like trying to steer a supertanker ship in a duck pond.

Guiding the titanic RV up the dirt road to Cloud Eight is like moving the Space Shuttle. One of the neighbors laughs and shakes his head as the massive rig slides backward down the mountain under its own crushing weight. I stand on the brakes, but all 10

wheels of the rig are locked up and sliding down the mountain. My neighbor laughs as I strain my eyes in the tow mirrors to make a winding turn as we slip backward down the road. Finally, the rig stops sliding. I push a shift lever on the floor of the old F-250, and the massive International Harvester diesel puts power to all four wheels. The Garret turbo sings like a jet engine as it packs air into the big cylinders. With a groan, the rig starts rolling up the hill again over the sand and ruts of the dirt road to Cloud Eight.

As the turbo-diesel growls up to Cloud Eight, we enter the next challenge, backing the massive trailer into the spot where Switch's little RV used to sit. It takes a team of spotters half an hour to guide me through a thirty-eight-point turn and slowly back the big rig into its new home.

"I can't believe you own this." my friend marvels at the massive RV now parked in his driveway. We both stand in awe of the luxurious house-on-wheels. The living room has more room than the little trailer we used to live in. It has a separate refrigerator and freezer, just like a real house.

It has an oven with range and microwave instead of the two little stove burners of our tiny RV. There's a hood/fan to pull the heat out of the room when I'm cooking for Wyatt in the summer. This is a new way of life.

Duane and Angela call it "The Rig." Wyatt calls it "Cloud Eight House." I now have my own bedroom, and Wyatt has a cool upstairs loft. It's like moving from our parking space-sized trailer into a real house.

Duane and Angela outfitted "The Rig" to perfection. It has thermostat-controlled central heat and air, and a whole-house water filter. It even has a garage where I can put a washing machine, so we can do laundry for the first time ever at Cloud Eight—no more running to the laundromat.

"The Rig" also has a few features that houses don't. There are vent fans that automatically open in summer to pull the heat out of the rig. If it starts to rain, the fans turn off and the vents close automatically. I wish the house at Cloud Nine had that!

And we have abundant room to grow. It's exactly what we need to prepare for the next stage of Wyatt's growth.

I decide to write Duane a letter because I want their family to know how much The Rig means to our family. I wondered how they might receive such a heart-felt note of thanks from the strangers who bought their old trailer. The response is overwhelming. Duane writes back instantly and says that they were planning to give the RV to charity, but when they prayed about it, they felt that they were being guided to find someone in need. They said, "Somebody needs The Rig."

I am moved to tears. Wyatt and I need The Rig.

Duane says his wife Angela keeps asking questions about us since we drove away with the rig. He gave me her email address so we could keep in touch. And that is how our Guardian Angel came into our lives.

Angela enthusiastically takes our little family under her wing. She sends the most beautiful prayers I've ever seen, for protection when I'm flying, and for healing when Wyatt's sick.

Every birthday or holiday, Angela, Duane, and Jenna Park put together a spectacular gathering, sometimes decorating the whole property at Cloud Eight or Cloud Nine. Angela and I share a laugh when I tell her we don't have room for all the toys they give us.

God bless the Park family. They have been relentlessly kind to us. It's just a reminder that it doesn't matter where you came from or how you live. Even if you live in a trailer, you can be loved and blessed.

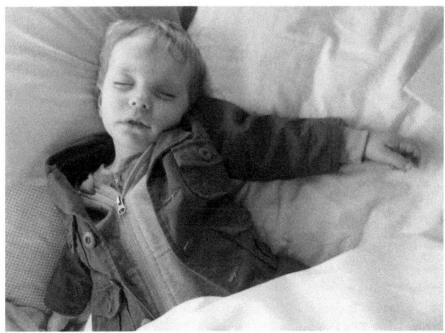

MAN VS. NATURE

THE LOVE AND KINDNESS OF Cloud Eight are a thousand miles away as I bounce against my seatbelt straps in the violent sky above *Deadliest Catch*.

I don't think I'm brave; I'm just too busy to think about it as I press the control levers on the Cineflex to smoothly zoom in to the men fighting rough seas and hurricane winds to get heavy crab pots out of the water.

The Cineflex holds my camera perfectly still and smooth as our helicopter somersaults in the storm.

"Oooh!" Our pilot sounds like he just got kicked in the stomach as a tornado of wind twists us toward the ocean and death. In a panic, our pilot pushes his control levers as far as he dares. If he pushes harder, the helicopter will break apart. But after applying every ounce of power the little aircraft has, we continue to fall out of the sky.

I pull my head out of the viewfinder and find that our windshield horizon has filled with wind-whipped seawater as we plummet. With the finesse and skill of a wizard, our pilot quickly wrestles the controls to avoid crashing without over-torqueing the little machine. The little Jet Ranger pushes with all its parts and every ounce of horsepower the screaming C-20 turbine can muster. I sink into my seat as we bounce just above the waves. This is the stormy weather *Deadliest Catch* is famous for.

I smoothly zoom out while the brave fishermen scramble on the crab boat below us. For them, the life and death wrestling match is just another day at the office.

"We're done!" Our pilot has seen God too many times. He pulls on the collective lever to climb into the storm and pushes his cyclic stick towards Dutch Harbor.

I waste nothing. Even as our pilot retreats to harbor, I pan and zoom to paint an ending to the violent scene on the crab boat. As the boat disappears in a frozen hurricane, our aircraft is pushed sideways and our skid flies across the camera frame. OK. That's the end of that shot.

I take a breath. The shot is over, but our violent struggle continues. Hopefully we can make it back in one piece. The Cineflex gyros and computers hold the camera perfectly still, but the skid now stretching across the image is writhing with each gust that smashes the little helicopter.

Very few Jet Rangers have flown in winds this violent. Everything around us is trying to murder us—the gale-force winds, the freezing Bering Sea, the low clouds, fog, and ice. We run with our tail between our legs to the tiny port of Dutch Harbor.

But our life and death adventure isn't over. Those crazy winds whirl over Ballyhoo Mountain and try to flip us upside down as our pilot tries to get us on the ground. "Whoa!" he yells as we're tossed like a child's toy. The cold gray landscape of Dutch Harbor blurs as we tumble in the violent winds. The two windsocks at the airport point in opposite directions as the hell-bent wind tosses us like a salad.

They say air flows like water, but the wind here is like a deadly Class VI river rapid, always trying to kill us. I think the wind is going to rip the rotor blades off the helicopter. I'll be amazed if we can land right-side up.

Our pilot wrestles with the wind to get our skids down without flipping over in the torrent, but the storm won't release us. The pilot wrestles all four control levers in different directions and get our skids on the icy ground. My stress-filled breath fogs the frozen window.

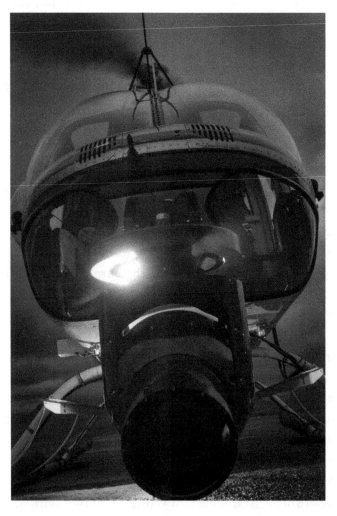

Our pilot twists his throttle grip to let the gas turbine cool down, but now he has a new problem. He has to get the blades stopped without chopping the tail boom off. The winds here never stop trying to kill us, even on the ground. Only when the blades stop turning are we finally out of danger.

I step out of the battle-tested Jet Ranger. My shirt is sticking to my body. I'm drenched in sweat. I take off my life-jacket and take a deep breath of salty air. I savor every stinging drop of frozen rain that hits my face. I need to cool down, too.

We slip and slide like circus clowns as we push the Jet Ranger across the ice and into the rickety old World War II hangar, but I don't mind the ice. I don't mind the cold. I don't mind the all-consuming salty mud of this place. I'm so happy to be alive after a typical day of flying here.

We head back to the Grand Aleutian Hotel, where I thank our pilot for keeping us alive.

In my hotel room, I get on my knees to thank God, who had just as much to do with it. Tomorrow, we'll do it again.

Year after year, I narrowly escape death and travel a thousand miles back to mainland USA and cell phone service.

A friendly voice lights up my phone. "You know, Dave, you can survive in that environment," says Nathan Crawford. Nathan is smarter than I, and he always thinks ahead. Now he's planning for the likely event of an emergency on the Bering Sea.

"I can survive?" I ask. As usual, Nathan's idea makes no sense to me. How can anyone survive in freezing seawater? Nathan patiently runs down a list of life-saving gear that military flight crews use in places like Afghanistan, and he tells me where to buy each item.

Nathan is a genius of things I don't understand, so I take his advice and buy everything on his list, which includes an insulated flame-proof flight suit, a helmet, and a satellite locator beacon. For the first time since *Deadliest Catch* began, I feel like I have a prayer of surviving an emergency on the Bering Sea. Thanks to my friend Nathan, the scariest environment is less scary.

ROAD RAGE

W HEN I GET BACK TO the City of Angels, there are no angels in sight—just angry people.

"Dad! Why is he doing that?"

The car in front of us is charging side-to-side on the highway. An enraged driver is trying to hit another car. The victim dodges to avoid being rammed into a wall, but the lunatic driver isn't through, he slams his wheel to the other side and charges again.

I dial 911, but there's no answer. I guess there're a lot of emergencies in the big city tonight.

I know this maniac is going to kill someone, so I dial 911 again as he charges at a family sedan full of kids. After the twelfth ring, a 911 operator finally answers.

"911, what's your emergency?"

Sky Falling
A Documentary

"I'm at I-210 and Waterman," I say. "There's a car weaving in traffic and trying to hit other cars. Whoah! Hang on! He just hit the wall." The crazy attacker leaves car parts and a trail of sparks in mid-air as he misses the family sedan and slams his own car into the center divider.

But the 911 operator couldn't care less. She seems more annoyed than concerned when I tell her the license plate and vehicle description. The 911 operator shows no interest even though we can see where the road-rage killer is going next with his smashed car.

I get nothing but awkward silence from the 911 operator. I guess she's busy.

I guess in the big city it's not a big deal. Murder and mayhem happen every day. The pressure of the asphalt jungle does this to otherwise normal people.

That's what makes Cloud Nine so special. It's in the LA metro, but at Cloud Nine there are no road-raging murders, no drive-by gangsters, just trees and birds. Instead of graffiti and razor-wire, our home is surrounded by clouds. Instead of police helicopters and sirens, we hear the wind inhaling and exhaling through a cloud forest.

When I walk outside at Cloud Nine, the forest is like a living orchestra. A cool breeze from the Pacific moves the tree leaves in a low whisper that reminds me of the sound of the ocean. Every color of bird sings a symphony that echoes through a mile-high cathedral of trees.

In a flash of color, the birds fly in all directions with a rhythm I've only heard in Sky Forest. Their wings make a gentle feathered drum-beat as they fly over our heads in the crisp mountain air.

It's a magic and unknown part of the LA desert where you can leave your doors unlocked, and children are free to roam in a cloud forest. We're in the middle of a desert, but somehow it rains and snows, causing Christmas trees to grow like weeds...

Sky Falling
A Documentary

LOST IN A STORM

THREE THOUSAND MILES AWAY, SEASON Two of *Deadliest Catch* starts in Dutch Harbor with film school class at 8:00 am. The whole crew meets so experienced shooters and producers can teach new crew members how to survive and make television on a Bering Sea crab boat.

The old salts teach new recruits how to manage when the boat rolls sideways on a thirty-foot rogue wave, and you have nothing to hold onto but your camera, which is hopefully still recording.

The school is just for people who shoot on boats. It has nothing to do with my helicopter, but I love to sit in class and try to learn how these amazing, energetic people make such a great show out of the violence and carnage of the Bering Sea.

Everyone here seems to have a reverence for the Bering Sea and the men who make their living on it. They share amazing stories of tired fishermen chopping ice off boats while hurricane winds and rogue waves try to send them to the bottom.

One night their horror stories echo in my head as the Bering Sea tries to send me to the bottom. Being offshore at night in our tiny helicopter is no picnic. In fact, when I look around, I see disaster in mid-swing. There are violent winds, darkness, and the near-zero visibility that kills many helicopter crews each year.

There is absolutely no margin for error here. Darkness swallows our helicopter en route to the fishing boats. Even Coast Guard pilots with advanced heated blades fear this place. Our pilot turns our little helicopter into winds that nearly flip us upside-down. We need only tip too far for a moment, and we will be lost at sea.

If you crash into the Bering Sea you have less than a minute before hypothermia takes you under.

I fearfully peer out my window from time to time, making sure I can still see the outline of the islands. The familiar shadow of Ballyhoo Mountain allows me to reassure myself that we can find our way home in the dark.

This is the same darkness that killed JFK Jr. It's the darkness that killed everyone in *The Perfect Storm.* The islands and seabed around us are littered with the rusting carcasses of aircraft that disappeared on a night like this.

The only thing that keeps us alive is the pilot's ability to discern up from down. Darkness and disorientation are sneaky sirens that beckon our pilot. He needs only to be seduced for a moment, and we'll be lost, sliding sideways and smashed, upside-down in the freezing waves.

As I capture a shot of the *Wizard* fishing in the darkness, I notice beautiful shafts of white light projecting in Captain Keith's forward sodium arcs. As usual, the Bering Sea shows us something beautiful and dangerous. The *Wizard's* lights look like the Bat Signal projected in front of the boat. But this signal is telling me something that I should have seen an hour ago...a storm is upon us.

Normally you can see a killer storm coming over the horizon and run to shore and safety, but at night, we see nothing except the brightly-lit crab boats. The boats are hovering in a black abyss of Bering Sea. In the back of our little helicopter, I bounce against my seatbelt straps as violent winds are getting stronger outside the thin Plexiglas of my window.

I'm always nervous here at night, but I notice our pilot's getting nervous too. "I didn't like that last turn," he says with desperation in his voice. I pull my head out of the Cineflex monitor, where Captain Keith's light beams are getting thicker with falling snow. I peer forward into the empty darkness that fills the pilot's windscreen, and I know why he didn't like that turn. As we crossed over the *Wizard*, he immediately suffered vertigo, the same phenomenon that killed JFK, Jr in his off-shore airplane crash. It's too dark. Our pilot can't see beyond the boat. And the darkness beyond the boat is hiding a monster.

"How much time to do we have left?" I ask.

He checks his fuel gauge. "I have about ten minutes left before we need to head back for fuel."

"Let's go back now," I say as the little voice in my head tells me we shouldn't be here.

"OK," says the pilot. "Let me see if I can figure out which way is home." When I hear this, the little voice in my head starts to scream. If the pilot can't figure out which way is home, we're doomed.

I snap my head to the window, looking for the familiar outline of Ballyhoo and Dutch Harbor, but now I can't see anything—just darkness. This tells me that we're in mortal danger. If I can't see the islands, then our pilot can't tell which way is up and where the ocean meets the sky. In other words, we're about to wander upside-down into the ocean like JFK Jr. did or slam into a mountain like many dead pilots have done on the islands around us.

While we were filming the boats, a blizzard moved in on top of us but was concealed by the darkness. We didn't know that we were getting into trouble. And now we're caught in a deathtrap. We've been doomed without our knowledge. The unforgiving

Bering Sea has us, and now the blizzard is hiding every reference our pilot needs to find his way back to Dutch Harbor.

I wish I was our director right now, sitting in front next to the pilot, unaware that we have a few minutes left to live. I peer over the director's shoulder. The front windscreen is pitch black. I can't see the mountains or the ocean. Now I know we're fucked. I make a mad dash to turn off all my equipment to keep illumination from distracting the pilot, who's blind-as-a-bat in the dark and stormy night.

I never turn off the Cineflex in flight, because it leaves the sensitive camera to bang against aircraft movements. But right now we're in such a predicament I can't even allow the orange glow of the power light to mess with the pilot's night vision as he tries to discern life from death in the darkness outside.

I scramble to unplug every electrical thing—anything that produces even the smallest light.

"Hey Dave, my monitor went off," our director calls out.

"I know," I say. "It's not coming back on, either."

I'm trying not to panic the director, who's our executive-level boss. Normally I'd cater to his comfort and wishes and keep his monitor on, but I can't talk to him right now. We're severely doomed, offshore in a storm, with no way to get home, and I don't have time to talk.

"Dave! Your equipment is blinding me. I can't see!" the pilot yells. But what equipment is he talking about? I already turned everything off! I'm sitting in pitch darkness in the backseat with dead camera equipment on my lap. Then it hits me. I look outside to the 206 tail, and I see a faint glimmer of green from our helicopter's navigation beacon. Looking up front I can see a green glow on the cockpit from the tiny light twenty feet behind the pilot's head.

Our pilot is so blinded by the darkness that the tiny green glow is overwhelming his eyes as he strains to see into the storm.

"It's your nav lights!" I tell him. "Turn your nav lights off!" He flips the switch and the light goes out. I'm now in complete darkness and thinking how I can possibly swim to shore after we crash into the Bering Sea. No one will know we've hit the water. It'll take over an hour for our colleagues to figure out we're overdue and where we could have crashed. And with no references, we could have crashed anywhere in the vast Bering Sea.

Each minute feels like an eternity. Hopefully we're still moving forward. I don't know. I look up front again and try to see something, anything, outside that will tell our pilot how to keep us in the air. Nothing. Oh wait, if I look to the side I can almost see the tiniest sparkle somewhere, many miles away. It's like trying to see the moons of Jupiter—just too tiny and dim to make out with anything but peripheral vision.

We've been flying like this for a while now. We're almost out of fuel. Each passing moment is a life and death barrier.

"What are you flying to?" I ask our pilot how he's steering us home.

"I don't know. I thought it was the lights of Dutch Harbor, but now I'm not sure."

That's it! We're dead. And I'm done with this death spiral. My little voice rises to a panic-stricken scream inside my head.

Remember when Rick questioned why I'd sit quietly in a crashing aircraft? God bless Rick. I'm a different person since he told me that, and now I make an executive decision.

"Turn around right now and go back to our boats!" I command.

I have no business commanding our pilot, who's older than me, smarter than me, and is the captain of our ship. I'm just a cameraman—literally a back-seat driver. My instructions will likely force us to run out of fuel.

The turn I just demanded may cause us to flame-out in the middle of the Bering Sea, but I don't care. If I'm going to crash, I want to crash next to our friends who can help us out of the water. We may flame out, but at least the pilot can use the lights of the boats to keep us right-side up until the engine quits.

Our pilot could tell me to shut up and let him fly the aircraft. After all, he's the pilot in command, and he's forgotten more than I'll ever know about surviving a storm like this. But he says nothing, just pulls hard on the cyclic stick and enters a sharp turn, back to our boats.

I know that I may have just killed us by turning us around and using up our remaining fuel, but my little voice says go to the light where our friends are.

Suddenly out of the darkness a plan drops into my head. I tell the director, "Call the skippers and tell them to turn on all their lights and steam toward Dutch Harbor." I tell the pilot, "The boats will give you a heading home."

The director has no idea how close to death we are. He casually asks which boat he should call on the radio.

The pilot takes a tremulous breath and screams, "Pick one!!!" I feel bad, because the fearful pitch of our pilot's voice tells the director that we are severely fucked.

But our director doesn't panic. Instead, he immediately swings into action with our first mayday radio call and asks the boats to stop what they're doing and set a course for Dutch Harbor with all lights on. This is probably very confusing to the boat captains who watched us leave a while ago and might assume we've been sitting on the ground refueling this whole time.

God bless Captain Sig Hansen of the *Northwestern*. He immediately recognizes the life and death struggle we're in. He answers on the radio as he throttles up his powerful engine and turns that big beautiful white boat toward Dutch Harbor. The darkness of the storm is impaled with long shafts of light from his powerful sodium arcs. Captain Sig shows us the way out of the deadly storm.

Our pilot and the little helicopter cling to Captain Sig's light like a moth to a flame. We're running out of fuel, but for now, we're saved by Sig's bright lights and quick-thinking.

Sig says, "Stay with me, I'll lead you all the way to the dock."

Our pilot gives some heart-stopping news to our director, who's waiting to be told how to answer Sig on the marine band radio. "Tell Sig we can't make it. We don't have enough fuel."

It's simple math. At top speed it'll take the *Northwestern* thirty minutes to get to Dutch Harbor. Because our fuel is so low, we'll flame out and crash before we ever see the lights of Dutch Harbor. We can't follow the Northwestern to the dock.

Our director relays the information to Captain Sig, and now everyone listening to marine radio knows our predicament. We're following Captain Sig and his lights, but we can't make it home at the speed of his boat. We're no longer lost in the dark, but we're almost out of fuel. We'll flame out and crash into the Bering Sea any second now. Sig doesn't hesitate. Somehow he knows exactly what to do. "OK. Just keep on this heading, it will take you right between the mountains to the harbor."

There's no time to talk. Our pilot pushes his cyclic stick full forward, and we accelerate into the darkness in front of Sig's boat. I watch out my backseat window as the last illumination from Sig's big stadium lights vanish behind us, and we're swallowed by darkness. I hope our pilot can keep us right-side up until the engine quits. It might help us get out of the sinking wreckage when the blades stop, and the cabin fills with seawater.

Pilots have a saying, "It's better to be on the ground and wish you were flying, than to be flying and wish you were on the ground." And this is what they mean. There is no refuge from this perfect storm. We can't land and live. No matter how we hit the water, death is certain. Death is quick.

Although we left the light from the *Northwestern* behind, we're still alive for the moment. Our Bell Jet Ranger's Allison C-20 gas turbine screams over my head as the blades chop away at the black-out blizzard. Deadly frozen waves reach up to our skids. If they can grab the tiniest part of our skids, we'll explode in the ocean.

Thank God I have the helmet and flight suit Nathan told me to wear. They might keep me alive for a minute or two.

You might think we could just swim for it, but the reality is it'll be like hitting a wall, upside down, at a hundred miles per hour. Because our emergency float system makes our little aircraft top-heavy, the machine will immediately sink upside down. The aircraft will squeeze us into a twisted pile beneath the crushing weight of the ice-cold Bering Sea.

It was a night like this that took down the Coast Guard

helicopter on Season One of *Deadliest Catch*. That mighty Coast Guard Jayhawk had two powerful engines, heated blades, and technology we could only dream of. And that Jayhawk was chewed up and swallowed by the Bering Sea.

But our little engine is still running as we career into the blizzard, pointing in the direction Sig gave us. We're alive for the moment. As I sit in the pitch-black passenger cabin, I move the Cineflex control off my lap and try to secure things around me in case we cartwheel into the ocean. It's a bit like arranging deck chairs on the Titanic, but it gives me something to do.

In the history of aviation, many have entered this scenario in small aircraft like ours. Most were never seen again. It took the US Navy a long time to find JFK Jr.'s body in the ocean, and he crashed in weather nicer than this.

I can't see anything outside except icy darkness. I hope we're getting closer to Dutch Harbor...

SKY FALLING
A Documentary

I've calmly faced death in aircraft around the world. Over the years, three dozen of my colleagues have died in situations like this one.

As the helicopter rotors pound into the night, I listen to the steady, comforting howl of the Allison turbine. The 206 has a rhythmic heartbeat, which tells me that although we're being pressed into a deadly abyss, we're still alive...God help our pilot and please guide us home...

"I can see town!" the pilot yells. I could kiss him as he calls out the lights of Dutch Harbor. We're saved! Those lights aren't just the distant sign of that weird, tiny little town. To me, the twinkling lights are life itself.

Captain Sig's careful guidance got us safely between the mountains and close enough to see the blessed lights of Dutch Harbor and that strange little airport.

Our pilot nurses the fuel-starved helicopter the last two miles to the airport. We land and slip-slide the little helicopter across the ice and into the old World War II hangar.

That rusting, dark, frozen hangar never looked so good.

If you've ever seen people kiss the ground on arrival, I can tell you why. I've never been so happy to see the icy, salty ground of Dutch Harbor.

When we step out of the helicopter, a behind-the-scenes camera crew rushes in with cameras and microphones. Apparently our crew made a mad dash to get to the airport to document our life and death struggle. They try to get me to talk on camera about the danger we endured, but I don't say a word. I've never talked about what happens in the sky above *Deadliest Catch* before.

The camera crew leaves and takes the director back to the hotel. The pilot and I are left alone with the helicopter in the old hangar. I lean into the pilot and ask, "When we were lost and turned around to go back to the boats, where do you think we were heading?"

The pilot scratches his head and says, "I don't know. But I think we were heading off-shore." So that's it. The storm had the pilot so confused that he was flying away from Dutch Harbor with no fuel left in his tank. We had nothing ahead of us but a thousand miles of Bering Sea. If we hadn't turned around and gone back to our boats, I wouldn't be here.

The Bering Sea had already claimed our helicopter with every soul on board. We won our lives back by turning around, going back to our boats, and asking our friends to light up the darkness. Thank God for our pilot's skill, that little voice in my head, Captain Sig Hansen, and our director, who did just the right thing at just the right time to save us from the darkness and death of *Deadliest Catch*.

MAGIC

Back in Los Angeles, I tell no one of our adventure on the Bering Sea. I just pick up Wyatt and start driving to Cloud Nine. Wyatt and I sit in bumper-to-bumper traffic for hours. But I love every second of the journey to Cloud Nine.

I think I can see steam rising off the foreheads of stressed-out city dwellers. To the angry motorists around me, LA traffic is a Hell-on-Earth nightmare, but I don't care. We might as well be on the Yellow Brick Road.

SKY FALLING
A Documentary

After fifty miles of standstill traffic, we finally inch our way onto Rim of the World Highway. Concrete buildings and razor wire magically turn into trees and wildflowers as we climb the mountain road toward Cloud Nine.

I once watched a crack addict shoot up. With the precision of a hacksaw machinist, he cut open a beer can and prepared the needle. His hand started to shake as he burned the powder into a liquid with a cigarette lighter. A self-deprecating smile crept across his lips as he looked up and said, "You see this? It's my body craving this shit." He held up his shaking hands for me to see how his body convulsed in anticipation of the ecstasy in that needle. I don't do drugs, but I know exactly how he feels. My whole being lights up when we turn the truck onto the winding road toward Cloud Nine.

Wyatt and I rock side-to-side as the old diesel roars up the mountain switchbacks. This highway is as close as you can get to helicopter flying. We bank side-to-side in a Jack and the Beanstalk rollercoaster that pulls us five thousand feet into the sky.

And now I have to stop the truck to take a picture.

"What are we doing dad?" Wyatt looks around to see why we've pulled over to the side of the road. We're three thousand feet in the air and only halfway to Cloud Nine.

"I have to take a picture buddy." I point out the window. "See those clouds? They're forming around the truck." The scene outside looks like *Lord of the Rings*.

Our pickup truck is half a mile up in the sky, but it doesn't look like a pickup truck. It looks like the Nautilus in a magic adventure. Clouds condense and swirl around us. Sunlight bounces off the moon and lights up the clouds. It's like standing in a surrealist painting.

Above the earthly sound of our diesel engine and traffic noise, I hear a chorus of angels singing in my head. Heaven and Earth come together on the side of the road.

I snap a picture and climb back in the truck. Magic is all around us, but, believe it or not, this is just a typical drive to Cloud Nine.

When we get to Cloud Nine, I feed Wyatt and get him into his pajamas. I light a fire in the fireplace and put a cartoon movie on the screen. We snuggle up on the couch watching the fire and the movie as the clouds swirl through the trees outside our windows.

As air conditioners hum in the dry desert city below, we watch the fire burn the chill off our mile-high house. When the movie is over, and Wyatt's gone to sleep, I walk outside to grab something from the truck, and I see something that stops me in my tracks.

I've walked in clouds before, but tonight is different. The clouds are illuminated by the full moon. I reach my hand out and touch the top of a cloud. The moon lights the forest like God's-own fluorescent bulb. It looks like a scene from a computer-generated fantasy movie. And it's pouring rain.

But I take one step forward, and it's not raining. What is this? I look down at dry ground under my Ozark Trail boots, but one step behind me, it's raining cats and dogs. I peer into the moonlit cloud and see the source of the rain—a seventy-foot Douglas fir tree. The rain is coming from the trees.

Down in the city of Los Angeles, a dry desert breeze blows as car horns and police sirens bounce off concrete buildings. But here in the cloud forest, the only sound is tree rain as the moonlit clouds stick to the trees and rain down onto the roots.

I raise my hands to heaven, close my eyes, and soak in the magic of my happy place.

Tomorrow I'll be in the city, and it might be a shitty day, but tonight I'm blessed.

SKY FALLING
A Documentary

DAY IN COURT

B ACK IN THE RAZOR-WIRED CITY, my child custody case comes to court, so I put on a suit and a smile and waltz into court without an attorney.

Wyatt's mom has a hyper-expensive Beverly Hills law firm, but even after she paid them $50,000, her lawyer can't seem to show up on time; the lawyer is late for appearances and *extremely* late for trial. So instead of a trial, we all sit around and wait for the lawyer to show up.

Wyatt's mom nervously checks her phone and whispers, "C'mon Jessica!" encouraging the lawyer who isn't here as we stare in awkward silence. How can a lawyer who charges so much for her time be late?

I thought this would cost them in court, but when the lawyer finally shows up, she and the judge start giggling about her legal fees and how they plan to stick me with them. Watching lawyers carve up my life and take all my money puts a knot in my stomach. It's not the merits of our case that matter. Right or wrong don't enter the equation, just how much they can get away with in legal fees. Now I can understand why the lawyer was late. If a judge can force people to pay your bill, you can show up whenever you want.

Mom's lawyer opens the trial and complains bitterly, because Wyatt and I live in a trailer at Cloud Eight. That's ironic, because our life with our friends at Cloud Eight is so good. We live in a trailer, but thanks to the Park family, it's a beautiful trailer. And thanks to our friends at Cloud Eight, we're surrounded by love (besides, mom sends Wyatt to Cloud Eight when she doesn't want him, so why is she complaining?)

Mom's lawyer scoffs at my way of life, saying, "Dad's living expenses are ridiculously low." That's right. Since I quit my job at Wescam, I don't know when I'll get paid, so I live within my means. I have to save money for the times I don't have work or paychecks.

But the lawyer and judge want money, so the judge takes my savings account and gives it to mom and her lawyer. God help me and Wyatt if I can't work.

I ask for nothing in court except what is best for my little one. I want Wyatt to have equal time with his mom and dad. But if I get equal time, then mom and her lawyer can't get as much money, so they fight tooth and nail to keep me away from Wyatt.

The judge refuses to give me equal time with Wyatt and fudges the numbers so that mom's high-priced lawyers get all of my savings, and I have to pay mom extra child support. He makes me pay more than the State of CA recommends, saying he doesn't think I'll spend time with Wyatt. What a scumbag. The judge also ignores evidence of substance abuse at mom's house. I've found Wyatt's mom completely intoxicated with our two-year-old son.

I get parking tickets at her house while banging on her doors and windows to try to get her to wake up from an intoxicated stupor and bring Wyatt out so I can get him out of there. I had to call the police to her house to kick in the door. She was disheveled and definitely under the influence. The police asked me, "Do you know what she's taking? We can't figure out why she's so out of it." Me neither. I don't know how she gets so intoxicated while caring for our toddler.

When mom drags to her door, she doesn't know what day it is, or if Wyatt has eaten breakfast. Meanwhile, Wyatt has *not* eaten breakfast. Wyatt actually stopped eating breakfast, because she wasn't feeding him or taking him to preschool. In spite of this evidence, the judge won't allow me to have equal time with our son.

Wyatt and I are screwed. And it's all about money.

When I pray about this, I ask God to connect those evil, greedy people to their darkness. My Christian friends might be horrified, but I know my prayer will be answered, and the bad guys will punish themselves. I've seen it before.

Mom's lawyer showed up late to our hearings, snapped up my life-savings, and then didn't bother to file the judge's ruling with the court. After five years and fifty thousand dollars, there's no court ruling on our case because mom's lawyers didn't file the documents like she was supposed to. Nuts.

The judge orders Wyatt to go with mom's nanny instead of me. I'm heart-broken and financially broken. Our Christian culture prizes forgiveness, but I'll never forgive this.

"Aww. You're so naive." A friend talks to me the way you'd address a child. My friend is right. I brought a picture book instead of a lawyer to a room full of sharks, and now I'm being eaten alive.

That judge won't see me again. But he'll work with mom's lawyers again and again. He made sure they got all of my money. As far as I can tell, that's the only rule in a court system run by lawyers.

If you think suing someone will get what you want, I'll let you in on a dirty little secret. The courts are not here for you. The courts are here for the lawyers. And lawyers want new cars.

A LIGHT BEFORE DARKNESS

Wyatt's mom never asks if I'll take him on her days. She just asks if I'm in town, because I ALWAYS take Wyatt if she doesn't want him.

I never make plans that can't include a two-year-old. If I'm not flying with Gibbs, I strap Wyatt into a backpack carrier, and he goes everywhere I go.

February 9, 2013, Wyatt and I are on Cloud Nine. I can see the concrete and razor wire of Los Angeles from our mountaintop, but up here a crisp wind blows white puffy powder into the air around us. It's the most beautiful, safe, and quiet environment I've ever seen. Wyatt and I bounce through the snow to our hearts' content.

The clouds form around the house and swirl through a winter wonderland. But unbeknownst to me, something is happening that will change our lives forever.

A HEARTBEAT AWAY

WHAT'S THAT NOISE? IT'S AN animal. No. It's a train. No! It's a telephone!

I wait for my eyes to focus on my watch. It's 6:00 am, and JT Alpaugh is on the phone. "Hello?" I try to sound intelligent while rubbing the sleep out of my eyes and looking around to remember where I am.

JT is the reporter I flew with over Hurricane Katrina. He sounds relieved. "Oh! Thank God you're OK! I'm in Air 7, flying to the scene of a helicopter crash!" JT sounds like he thought I was killed in the crash. He seems relieved to hear that I'm alive, but also seeking answers as a journalist. I say, "I don't know anyone flying in that area. I'll see if I can find out who it was and call you back." I hang up the phone and text my flying friends. I hope they're all ok. Maybe one of them knows who crashed last night.

No one texts back. It's Sunday morning, and I doubt if they're even awake yet. As I sit waiting to hear from my friends, I scroll through the list of messages to see which of them have phones showing signs of life. All their phones report "message delivered," except for my closest friend and work partner, Gibbs. I have a sinking feeling when his phone doesn't respond.

I'm nervous to call his house because his fiancé might be worried by my early-morning phone call, but I need to know. I dial his number and hope that Gibbs will answer the phone, and we can have one of our typical arguments. But Gibbs doesn't answer. She picks up the phone. She doesn't say hello, just screams, "Why are you calling here?!"

Before I can say a word, she knows why I'm calling. I'm calling because of something we're both afraid of.

I take a deep breath and try to comfort her. "It's OK. What's going on?" From her panicked tone, I already know what's going on.

"Gibbs is on a shoot, but he didn't come home last night. I haven't heard from him," she worries out loud.

My heart sinks. We both immediately know what happened last night, but don't want to accept it. I try to reassure her. "Don't worry. Let me make some calls and get some information. I'll call you back."

I make some calls. "Yeah, it's weird," says one person. "Gibbs flew away yesterday, but that's the last we saw of him. The helicopter never came back, and his Jeep is still sitting here."

That's not good. Gibbs didn't come back in the helicopter.

Finally, I get hold of our friend who owns the helicopter that Gibbs is flying. "It was our boy," says the distraught aircraft owner. I don't want to hear what I'm told about the crash. I take a deep breath as the shock comes over me like an icy rogue wave. I lost my big brother last night. He died in a pile of twisted helicopter parts.

I don't bother calling Gibbs' fiancé back. Instead, I get little Wyatt out of bed, put warm clothes on him, and load Switch's RV. I shift the pickup into four-wheel drive low, and we slide through the snow. I drive us down to Gibbs' house, where I'll camp out and help his fiancé with the difficult days ahead.

Gibbs and I entered the sky a thousand times. We flew together so often that when people learn of Gibbs' accident, they assume I died too.

TELL YOUR FRIEND GIBBS I SAID, "THANK YOU."

"WHY ARE YOU DOING THIS?" a friend asks as I switch my family cell phones to Verizon.

I explain. "I want to take over Gibbs' cell phone so I can keep his voice on the voicemail." Gibbs has Verizon. I have AT&T, but I switch all my phones to Verizon so that when I dial his number, I can still hear his voice on the greeting.

Gibbs was taken so suddenly that none of his loved ones got to say goodbye. Now I maintain his phone so friends and family can hear his voice and leave him a message.

The sound of Gibbs' voice makes me smile. I miss talking to him. I know he's gone, but I wish I could talk to him again, just like old times, for just a minute…

I thought I could handle Gibbs' death. I know the dangers of flying cameras. But after his accident, I've become a grief-stricken mess. I put on a brave face in front of his fiancé, but from time to time I slip into his garage where no one can see. I wish Gibbs was here to open his old Jeep doors and put on easy-listening jazz like he used to do. I wish he was here to give me shit with every breath he takes. But Gibbs is gone. He left without saying goodbye. There are no funny insults. The music is gone. His garage is empty and cold. Gibbs' friends are in the next room helping Cindy. No one can see me here. So I lean onto his old Jeep and cry my eyes out.

Gibbs and I gave each other shit relentlessly for 18 years. He once called me an "uncultured baboon," which still makes me laugh out loud because, as usual, Gibbs was half-right.

157

Gibbs was the hardest-working, most kind-hearted man I ever met. Since his death, I'm feeling depressed. The world is a dull, flavorless place that I lumber through.

I'm dragging through an airport on my way to a helicopter shoot, and as I drift past the gift shops and bars, I hear a voice telling me to call my friend Aaron and talk to his wife Melanie, who's a child custody attorney.

"No." I say. "I'm not doing that."

The voice in my head is driving me nuts, though.

"Call Melanie!"

"No! I'm not calling her. It's Sunday!" I say out loud.

Aaron's wife Melanie helped me with my child custody case on her personal time, giving advice. I don't want to bother her on a weekend, when I'm sure she's trying to not think about child custody cases, but the voice keeps saying that I must call her.

"Call Melanie and talk to her about Wyatt."

"No! The last thing she wants to hear today is work stuff. I'm not calling her. It's Sunday!" I look around, but there's no one — just me and a crowd of strangers, making their way through a bustling airport. The airport is full of normal people who can't hear the voice in my head.

The voice falls silent. Good. I won. The surreal argument ends, and I got the last word.

"Tell your friend Gibbs that I said, "Thank you." Angela Park is on the phone, but not to ask about Wyatt or pray for my trip, like she normally does. What she says makes no sense. She never met Gibbs and doesn't know him, except that he was in the news because he died in a helicopter crash. But now Angela's going on about David Gibbs, and she says one of the most shocking things I've ever heard anyone say. "Did Wyatt's mom get arrested?"

"What?!"

"Go check your email."

I check my email and find a criminal mugshot of Wyatt's mom. She looks like Hell.

"Where did you find this?" I ask.

"Your friend David Gibbs sent it to me."

Angela says Gibbs sent the mug shot to her today, but I don't know how that's possible. David Gibbs died in a helicopter crash. How can Gibbs send anything? He's dead.

I suddenly remember that my ex's car mysteriously disappeared last year. And when I dropped Wyatt off at her house, she looked like she'd been hit by a train. She even had a black eye. She acted nervous and stammered, "I love the Nissan, but it broke down, so I had to buy a new car."

I didn't have a clue what was going on. My friends taught me not to worry about her well-being anymore, so I didn't ask about her new car or her black eye. And I'm not very smart, so I missed the obvious signs that she did something awful with the car I gave her.

The real story came and went without my knowledge months ago. I never would have known about her drunken car crash and DUI conviction. This information has implications for me and Wyatt. Now I can go back to court and make them give me the only thing I asked for: equal time with my son.

I ask Angela how she found this secret information, about mom's drunken car crash and DUI arrest.

"I don't know," she says, "but your friend David Gibbs sent it to me."

I'm flabbergasted, but then I remember the weird argument I had with that voice at the airport. I guess Gibbs told Angela something, too, but she didn't argue with him, like I did. She took his advice. And now I have my ex's mugshot and criminal arrest record.

So I bring mom's mugshot and arrest record to a child custody attorney. She looks at the police report and says, "Wow! Mom was VERY intoxicated." The attorney pauses and thinks about it for a long minute, searching the heavens for what to do about the case. Suddenly it hits her. "I know what to do," she says triumphantly. "I think you should talk to an attorney who specializes in dealing with cases like this. Have you ever heard of a lawyer named Melanie Mandel?" (Aaron's Wife, Melanie)

When I hear this I burst into tears. David Gibbs already told me to call Melanie Mandel. Gibbs came to me as an annoying voice inside my head. He told me over and over, "Call Melanie and talk to her about Wyatt." But, as usual, we argued...

Gibbs knew that the judge ignored evidence of mom's intoxication while caring for Wyatt. In spite of this, the judge took Wyatt away from me and put him with mom's nanny. He then ordered me to pay excess child support and lawyer fees.

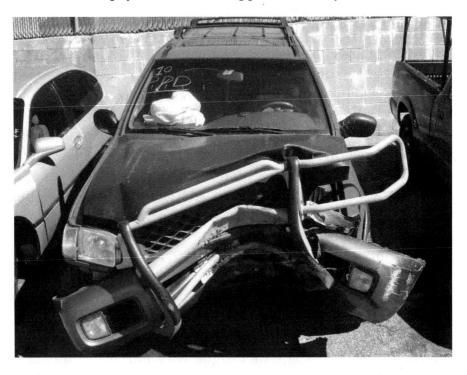

I only asked for equal time, but Wyatt and I got screwed. And according to the calendar, mom's drunken crash happened on one of her days with Wyatt. Thank God Wyatt wasn't killed.

I could've lived my whole life without knowing she got drunk and pretzeled my old car, but now I'm armed with Gibbs' revelation. So I pay a visit to Pasadena Police Department and look up mom's record. It contains a receipt from Master Towing in Pasadena, so I l drive to the address and peer over the junkyard fence. In the impound yard I finally find what Gibbs is talking about—my old car, smashed to Hell. One of the junkyard workers asks what I'm doing. I point to the twisted steel and say, "That's my old car. My ex said it broke down, but I just found out she was arrested for DUI."

Behind the police labels my old steering wheel has an exploded air bag dangling out of it. The airbag probably gave mom the black-eye. I ask the junkyard guy if I can buy my old car and fix it.

"Nah bro. It can't be fixed..." he says. "Your ex totaled it."

He kindly lets me take pictures from behind the fence. Then he says something interesting. "It's weird that your car is still here, bro. Normally, we sell them at auction by now."

If they'd sold my car at auction, I'd never have seen what my ex-girlfriend did in her drunken smash. Thank God for these pictures (and Gibbs).

Now, I can use Gibbs' information about mom's arrest to demand more time with Wyatt. Wherever Wyatt and I go, the rest of our lives will be better because Gibbs cared enough to break some rules and send me a message. This parting gift reminds me of the message I received from my mom after her death.

Once again, I find myself typing through tears. I can't believe a man I knew for eighteen years as "Dave Number Two" could turn my life on a dime after his death. Please don't tell him I said this. I'll never hear the end of it. But Gibbs really was "Dave Number One," and I always looked up to him. He helped me earn a living and made me laugh every day for 18 years. And then he told Heaven to wait so he could go back down to Earth to give me a hand with something I don't know how to fix.

God bless you David Gene Gibbs, the hardest-working, most kind-hearted man I ever met.

DAVE NUMBER TWO

GIBBS SAW THE HELL I went through just to be told I can't spend time with Wyatt. I think if people know the story, they'll understand why Gibbs went so far to set things right after his death. I'm not allowed to spend equal time with Wyatt. A bunch of money-loving lawyers got in the way. People who know better chose evil and greed over doing the right thing for me and Wyatt. I think Gibbs has another outcome in mind. Thanks to Gibbs' message, I now have hope that Wyatt and I will have more time together in the future. It's going to be an interesting year.

David Gibbs told me where to point my camera for eighteen years. When I told him I'm in charge, he'd say, "You sit in your little seat and point that camera where I tell you!" We had the same argument every day at work, and I just realized something that makes me uncomfortable. Gibbs is gone, but he's still telling me what to do.

Now, I've been asked to speak at Gibbs' funeral. For eighteen years I tried to get the last word in, but now I don't want the last word. I miss the way Gibbs used to interrupt me and remind me of whatever stupid thing I did this morning.

But Gibbs isn't here. I'll do all the talking, and it's not as easy as I thought.

"Start with one of your stories," says a friend of mine.

"Okay," I say.

But I've never told a story to a crowd before. I thumb through my notes, which now look like a rambling mess.

I take a nervous step toward the microphone at Gibbs' funeral.

That's a big crowd. I try to look calm while swallowing the lump in my throat. Cathedral spotlights are heating up my forehead. I loosen my tie, which felt fine before, but I must have tied too tightly. Three hundred people stare at me with hungry eyes. I know they want me to say something hopeful, but I don't know how to do this.

I planned a joke to ease the tension, but I nervously stammer and forget half the joke. It's not funny. Not a single person laughs. Everyone is staring at me. The spotlight feels hotter in the awkward silence after my bombed-out joke. Public speaking is not what I do. But I hear a voice that says something I already know. I need to tell people about my friend.

Wait a minute. There's something familiar about this. I was told about this before it happened.

"You're a dufus Dave. You could screw up a two-car funeral," said David Gene Gibbs, every day of our flying career. And, you know what's funny? He was right. I'm screwing up his funeral.

But since I already screwed up in front of his crowd, the pressure's off. So I lean into the microphone, and I tell the story of a man who reprimanded me every day for 18 years. "In the two decades that I knew David Gibbs, we didn't have one normal conversation. In fact, most days, he threatened to beat me to death."

"His name was David Gibbs, but I never called him that, just Dave Number Two.

"He used to refer to the fingers of his clinched fist as individual people who were going to kill me. Gibbs would say, 'I'm going to land this helicopter and beat you for a week!'" The awkward silence is replaced by the sound of several hundred people snickering. Pained expressions soften with smiles as the congregation remembers the comical warmth of David Gibbs. Now they're laughing, and they're nodding, because they know I'm telling the truth about our friend.

The truth is, David Gibbs threatened me a thousand times when we flew over *The Amazing Race* and the Super Bowl, but he never landed the helicopter to beat me up. He was, in fact, the most kind-hearted man I ever met. He gave me more opportunities than anyone in my career. And he always threatened to beat me up, because he knew it made me laugh. He made me laugh every day for 18 years. In fact, I can honestly say that Dave Number Two never entered a room without going out of his way to put a smile on my face.

And, now I must admit another truth. "Dave Number Two was really Dave Number One."

I'm trying not to cry, but the best I can do is half-crying, half-talking. Suddenly I notice that people in the crowd are crying too. I think I just saw 300 handkerchiefs come out of purses and pockets. If there's a dry eye in the room, I can't find one. I suppose people are crying because they know how much I miss my friend and his daily "death threats."

When I finish my speech in front of Gibbs' funeral crowd, the silence is broken by people clapping. But that's not right, you're not supposed to applaud after someone's death. Oh well, if you invite me to speak, I can promise you won't have a normal funeral. I suppose people are clapping because I didn't talk about Gibbs' death; I told the story of the wonderful life I had with my friend. It started when the nicest man I ever met climbed into a helicopter with me and said he, "wanted to enter the sky."

As I walk out of the church, people I've never met ask to shake my hand. It's nice to feel the love they still have for Gibbs. Everyone looks up as the sky fills with aircraft flying a salute to our friend. My eyes fill with tears as, one-at-a-time, each pilot flies to honor David Gibbs. I recognize all the planes and helicopters; I've flown in all of them, usually with Gibbs on the controls and yelling at me. But as the last helicopter passes, here comes something that I've never seen before. A fighter jet screams toward us with one of Gibbs' colleagues at the controls. But the pilot doesn't fly like the other pilots. He has something special planned.

The jet pilot flips a switch and a special fluid is injected to his engines, causing them to leave a trail of smoke behind as he accelerates through the air. As he zooms over our heads, in a salute to David Gibbs, he snaps the yoke to one side and rolls upside down, cutting a circle in the sky, and then he pushes the throttles full-forward in a move known as "balls-to-the-wall." The air fills with thunder. Three hundred people let out a collective gasp. The ground under my feet trembles as the power of two thousand horses push the jet straight up into the sky.

The jet rockets out of sight in the same way that Gibbs left me, with a breathless mixture of good vibrations. It's a fitting tribute to a man who threatened to beat me up every day, but never laid a hand on me. He went out of his way to make me smile, and then he was gone.

COMING UP

FTER GIBBS' DEATH, I LOSE a number of other colleagues who crash while flying for TV and movies. One of them is Hollywood movie pilot Alan Purwin. Alan is the visionary who spear-headed development of the equipment I use every day. He's the pilot who flew me over Hurricane Katrina with his company's game-changing technology. Sadly, Alan died in an airplane crash while he was working on a Tom Cruise movie.

I'm no better than Gibbs or Alan Purwin. I'm no smarter than my colleagues, who died while flying for TV shows and movies. The dirty little secret is, I'm the least smart among them. I've flown straight into blizzards. I've spun to the ocean. I've hit the ground more than once, and I should have known better. But each time I had help from above.

"Hey Dave, I want to fly with you in Alaska." A journalist is on the phone. He says he wants to do a story about my flying career over *Deadliest Catch*.

"Great." I say. "C'mon up to Alaska. You'll need a class in underwater crash survival."

"Underwater crash survival?" He sounds like a man who's hungry but lost his appetite. I can hear the enthusiasm drain from his voice as I explain the number of people who've died in the freezing waters of *Deadliest Catch*.

When I tell him of my near-death experiences in our helicopter over the Bering Sea, he says he's changed his mind; he doesn't want to go. And then he pauses. There's an awkward silence as he takes a deep breath and asks, "Why do you do it?"

It's a good question. Why, after Gibbs' death, do I continue?

Why, after Alan Purwin crashed, do I still fly in the same conditions that killed them both? I don't know, but I have a feeling.

"I feel that humans are built for adventure," I say. "We're not made to play it safe." Maybe that's why I've flown a thousand times since Gibbs died, and I've done every dangerous thing that killed Gibbs and other friends who are no longer with us. It took me a long time to realize how this makes me different from other people. Only in cataloging my adventures did I come to understand it. Although Gibbs died in a helicopter crash, he lived more in a single day of "painting his canvas" than most men ever will.

President Reagan spoke of astronauts who reached for the stars but died in a fiery crash. He said they "'slipped the surly bonds of earth' to 'touch the face of God.'" I don't exactly know what that means, but I know that human beings are simply not made to spend life in the safety of cubicles.

When I dealt with lawyers who successfully kept me away from my son, they laughed. I think they laughed because when they left the courtroom, they drove to gated communities, paid for by me and other people they victimize. They live a comfortable life, free of consequences. No matter how much they lie, cheat, and steal, they won't be harmed.

But I believe that every time they take joy from a child, those lawyers die a little inside. They may live behind golden fences, but I think they're trapped in there. Their spirits are dying behind fences that keep the danger out.

I may live a dangerous life, but I'm really *living*.

When given a choice, I hope that you'll do what Gibbs did. I hope that you'll decide not to play it safe, but to push those balls to the wall. Find a way to enter your sky and paint your canvas.

I've been painting the sky for twenty-three years. My work is beautiful and dangerous. But there's more to me than my work. There's a story I haven't told you yet.

It is a story bigger than the Super Bowl or *Amazing Race*, and it takes place in my beloved hometown of Sky Forest, CA. The story involves children at our town school bus stop who were waiting for the bus one day when something bad happened.

We all saw it. We knew that it was murder. But we were told to keep silent about it. We were told that we'd be killed if we asked questions or called attention to the crime. Most people are smart enough to heed warnings from powerful people. As long as they can keep the story a secret, the bad guys can keep making money illegally at the school bus stop.

As long as no one makes a scene, the bad guys can keep getting away with murder. Many people have been hurt by the school bus secret. Some have been killed. But because no one speaks of it, the crimes continue.

But you know me. I'm "thick as a brick" sometimes. Smart thinking never stopped me before. So fasten your seatbelt and get ready for a wild ride. The school bus is the reason I wrote the book you're holding in your hands. That's right. Book One is a prequel.

The real adventure is about to begin.

Book Two, *HELP FROM ABOVE: What Lies above the Clouds* is the true story of what happened at the school bus stop in a little town. It is the story they told me never to tell.

Book Two is not just a book. It's a first-ever, grass-roots effort to bring down an organized crime ring. As usual, I'll need a lot of help. I hope you'll take a risk and come with me on a dangerous mission. I could use a hand, writing a happy ending for the kids at the school bus stop.

My name is David Alan Arnold. And this is my continuing story.

SKY FALLING
A Documentary

HELP FROM ABOVE
What Lies Above the Clouds

HELP FROM ABOVE
What Lies Above the Clouds

If you like the stories in this book, check out the
pictures and videos that go with them:

Instagram: @airbornecamera

Twitter: @DavidAlanArnold

Facebook: David Alan Arnold

YouTube: David Alan Arnold
https://www.youtube.com/channel/
UChvtDqFS1Uydyl615efR23A?view_as=subscriber

Website: www.DavidAlanArnold.com

The Adventure Continues…

Coming Soon:

HELP FROM ABOVE

BOOK TWO

WHAT LIES ABOVE THE CLOUDS — A TRUE STORY

EMMY AWARD-WINNING
HELICOPTER CAMERAMAN OF DEADLIEST CATCH

— HELP FROM ABOVE BOOK 2 —

WHAT LIES ABOVE THE CLOUDS

A TRUE CRIME STORY

Now A
DOCUMENTARY
SERIES

DAVID ALAN ARNOLD

ACKNOWLEDGEMENTS

A Little Help from my Friends

When I struggled to build a small barbecue grill, my friend Nathan realized how clueless I was. But, he pitched in to help me figure it out. This book is no different. I couldn't figure it out by myself.

Thank you to Charles Ricciardi. Charles has been helping me for years. He gave me one thousand, eighty-five corrections. That's how many mistakes I made on this book. Only a true friend will take time to correct you over a thousand times. If the book makes sense, it's mostly because of Charles.

When Lucetta Zaytoun read an early draft, she said, "Dave, do you know what a paragraph is?" I guess my grammar needs a lot of work. So, I did my best to fix every paragraph.

Fredda Rose knows a lot about books. When she read my book, she said, "Dave, you should write two books!' I took her advice. I've written two books. Book Two is coming next.

Jeff Conroy is one of the creators of Deadliest Catch. He kindly spent hours, reading my material and helping me re-work until it made sense.

Decker Watson is an Executive Producer of Deadliest Catch. He said, "Dave, you should write three acts, like a movie." So I took his advice. You're reading the first act. There will be two more books or acts in the Help From Above Series.

Steve Harrison owns the Quantum Leap Academy. He said, "Dave, will you do public speaking?" So, now I do public speaking. If you know who I am, outside this book, it's because of Steve Harrison. Steve taught me how to get a story out, into the world. Steve's coaches helped me every step of the way: Geoffrey Berwind, Brian T. Edmondson, Martha Bullen, Raia King, Tamra Richardt, Chris Kennedy. Thanks to the entire staff at Quantum Leap. And thank you to my fellow students at Quantum Leap, like Jen Coken, who travelled across the country to help me.

Debra Englander is a Quantum Leap Coach. She took one look at my book and said, "Do you know what an Introduction is?" Wow! I guess my Introduction was pretty lame. So, I stopped what I was doing and re-wrote the Introduction.

Jack Canfield is co-author of Chicken Soup for the Soul. When he read my new Introduction, he said, "You're a fabulous writer. That is excellent, engaging, powerful, emotionally moving stuff." Thanks Jack! But, it only looks that way because Debra, my coaches and friends kept pushing me to make it better.

Thank you to every person on this list and those I forgot to mention. I can do big things if people help me. To write this book, I needed a little help from my friends.

ABOUT THE AUTHOR

David Alan Arnold is an Emmy-Award-Winning Cinematographer.

He has flown around the world for movies like James Bond and hit TV shows, like Amazing Race, Deadliest Catch, World Series and Super Bowl.

For twenty years, he never talked about his work, until writing this book…

CPSIA information can be obtained
at www.ICGtesting.com
Printed in the USA
BVHW040337080221
599614BV00026B/548